Taking
A
Sex History

Taking
A
Sex History
Interviewing and Recording

Wardell B. Pomeroy
Carol C. Flax
Connie Christine Wheeler

THE FREE PRESS
A Division of Macmillan Publishing Co., Inc.
NEW YORK

Collier Macmillan Publishers
LONDON

THE FREE PRESS
A Division of Macmillan Publishing Co., Inc.
866 Third Avenue, New York, N.Y. 10022

Collier Macmillan Canada, Ltd.

Library of Congress Catalog Card Number: 81-67164

Printed in the United States of America

printing number
1   2   3   4   5   6   7   8   9   10

Library of Congress Cataloging in Publication Data

Pomeroy, Wardell Baxter.
  Taking a sex history.

  Includes index.
    1. Sex counseling.   2. Medical history taking.
  3. Interviewing in psychiatry.   I. Flax, Carol C.
  II. Wheeler, Connie Christine.   III. Title.   [DNLM:
  1. Sex behavior.   2. Medical history taking.   HQ 21
  P7853t]
  RC556.P65   155.3   81-67164
  ISBN 0-02-925370-5   AACR2

Contents

ACKNOWLEDGMENT

We thank the Kinsey Institute, especially its director Paul H. Gebhard, for allowing us to divulge the Kinsey coding system as well as the interviewing techniques that form the basis of this book.

ABOUT THE AUTHORS

Wardell B. Pomeroy (Ph.D. Columbia University) joined Alfred C. Kinsey at the Institute for Sex Research in 1943. One of Kinsey's chief collaborators on *Sexual Behavior in the Human Male* (1948) and *Sexual Behavior in the Human Female* (1953), he later became the Institute's director of field research and also served as co-author of its third and fourth studies, *Pregnancy, Birth and Abortion* (1958) and *Sex Offenders: An Analysis of Types* (1965). His other books include *Boys and Sex, Girls and Sex*, and *Dr. Kinsey and the Institute for Sex Research*. Since 1976, Dr. Pomeroy has held the academic deanship of the Institute for Advanced Study of Human Sexuality, San Francisco.

Carol C. Flax (Ph.D. New York University) teaches at the Columbia University College of Physicians & Surgeons, at Hunter College, and at the New School. Director of the Columbia University Seminar on Human Adaptation and former coordinator of the Sexual Therapy Program at Columbia Presbyterian Medical Center, she writes, consults, and lectures widely on sexual disorders and therapies and is co-author (with Earl Ubell) of *Getting Your Way—The Nice Way: A Guide for Parents and Grown-up Children*. Dr. Flax also maintains a private practice in New York City specializing in the treatment of sexual problems.

Connie Christine Wheeler (Ph.D. candidate New York University) is a sex researcher and private practitioner in psychotherapy and counseling in New York City and former executive director of the society for the Scientific Study of Sex. Co-editor of the anthology *Progress in Sexology*, she is a delegate and significant contributor to the biennial international congresses of sexology.

1

Introduction

There are probably few people in the world today who have not heard of Dr. Alfred C. Kinsey's work in sex research. Hundreds of thousands of people, and surely the majority of sex therapists, counselors, educators, and researchers have read of Kinsey's findings in the books which he and his colleagues at the Institute for Sex Research produced, during his lifetime and later,* or in the summaries published in the media or prepared by later popularizers.

Far fewer people know that Kinsey made at least two other major contributions to sex research and sex therapy. In the course of his investigations, he developed a technique of eliciting detailed and accurate information from an enormous variety of subjects regarding their most intimate experiences—experiences which many of them had never before verbalized to another person. And the need to record their responses in a manner that ensured confidentiality and at the same time made the information instantly retrievable for purposes of research or therapy led him to devise an ingenious and highly practical system of coding the responses.

It is the purpose of this book to describe and explain the interviewing and coding system used by Kinsey and his colleagues, to provide an aid to a later generation of scholars and practitioners.

We recognize that the method of eliciting information is more important than the method of recording it; there can be other methods of recording data, but hardly better methods of eliciting information in a most sensitive area. Accordingly, the emphasis in this book is on the interviewing techniques—what questions to ask, in

*A.C. Kinsey, W.B. Pomeroy, and C.E. Martin, *Sexual Behavior in the Human Male* (Philadelphia: W.B. Saunders, 1948); A.C. Kinsey, W.B. Pomeroy, C.E. Martin, and P.G. Gebhard, *Sexual Behavior in the Human Female* (Philadelphia: W.B. Saunders, 1953).

what order, how to phrase them, and so forth—but because in practice the responses are coded simultaneously, the interviewing techniques are presented in the framework of the recording instrument. The reader should not, however, lose sight of the primary importance of the interviewing techniques.

The method of taking a sexual history presented here is a face-to-face, personal, structured interview. In other words, each interview is conducted in person rather than through a mailed questionnaire; in most cases only two people are present at the interview—the subject and the interviewer;* and the interviewer administers a predetermined sequence of questions, each intended to elicit a brief and quite explicit response. Special aspects of interviewing on sexual topics are considered in detail in Chapter 3 and illustrated throughout the book.

Previous researchers have generally preferred a questionnaire comprised of objective questions and scales with fixed or closed answers. This can be mailed or administered in person to individuals or groups, and if the items are skillfully written, such an instrument can yield an abundance of data. Since no special skills are needed to administer a questionnaire, it can be given to a large number of respondents within a defined time and is therefore economical. When it is distributed personally rather than mailed, a high rate of completion is virtually guaranteed. The responses are relatively easy to handle statistically, and the instrument lends itself to computer programming.

The personal, face-to-face interview, on the other hand, must be administered by someone well schooled in the techniques of interviewing, is not suited to groups, and is costly to administer and to interpret. This method, however, avoids the major drawback of the questionnaire. Whether mailed or personally administered, questionnaire respondents may fail to understand the meaning of a question, and this failure may lead to invalid responses and ultimately to invalid findings. A personal interview allows both the subject and the interviewer to ask for clarification of puzzling questions or responses. The mailed questionnaire frequently has a low percentage of returns, necessitating costly and time-consuming follow-up, and in the long run the results may not be worth the time, effort, and expense involved. Finally, the predetermined questionnaire gives the interviewer no opportunity to pursue the details of unusual or unexpected responses, so that the bare statistical results may not reveal the richness of personal experience.

In the method described in this book responses are recorded throughout the interview on a single sheet of $8\frac{1}{2} \times 11$ paper which is ruled into "blocks" to correspond with the twenty-four major aspects of background or behavior that are of interest to the interviewer, from health to zoophilia (see Figure 1–1, p. 4). All responses are coded according to a simple and relatively brief list of symbols which derive their meaning from their position on the recording sheet. For example, an **M** can indicate mother, masturbation, Methodist, or marriage, depending on its location on the recording sheet. The code is therefore called a "position" code.

The techniques presented here of course have specific reference to sexual behavior and attitudes, but the principles underlying the Kinsey approach to interviewing and coding can easily be adapted to other areas of inquiry in a vast number of disciplines. A physician could use the position code to explore eating habits in relation to

*On rare occasions an observer is present—for example, for diagnostic evaluations, in conjoint therapy, or to check on the accuracy of the interviewer's recording methods or the reliability of his or her subjective interpretations of a person's responses.

cancer, by devising a block of questions suited to this issue and then recording the responses. Similarly, a sociologist could adapt the code to an exploration of housing problems; an anthropologist could use it to elicit details of tribal relationships, and so on. The usefulness of the model is limited only by the imagination of the interviewer.

In the chapters that follow, we deal first with the question that virtually every interview subject asks or, it can be assumed, at least ponders in the course of giving his or her sexual history: "Am I normal?"

Chapter 3 presents some general pointers about interviewing on sensitive topics, derived from extensive experience in taking sexual histories. These are not intended as inflexible rules but rather as tried and true techniques that facilitate the interviewer's task. The chapter will also explain in advance some of the interviewer's remarks in the question-and-answer sequences we have used to illustrate the body of the text. For example, why does the interviewer frequently say "good" or "fine" to a respondent who has just described his or her sexual experiences with prepubertal children or with animals?

We introduce the recording sheet developed by Kinsey and his associates in Chapter 4 and offer some general principles of coding, including a glossary of the symbols used most frequently. Special symbols used in recording specific blocks of information are discussed under the relevant block.

Each of the subsequent chapters focuses on one of the twenty-four areas of information elicited in the sexual history. The final two chapters address the separate inventories given to people with extensive involvement in homosexuality and in prostitution.

We have found that the sexual history generally takes one to two hours to elicit, although the time can be expanded or contracted to suit special purposes. It can, for example, be covered in a fifty-minute therapy session, although obviously this brief session will not allow for great detail. An interview conducted for research purposes generally takes at least an hour and a half.

FIGURE 1-1. Sex history interview form

2

"Am I Normal?"

Mores in our culture have made discussion of personal sexual matters difficult for many people, including a good many professionals. Therefore few interviewees will have any accurate notion of how their own behavior patterns differ from or conform to the average, the typical, or, as they are more likely to phrase it, the "normal" pattern. Most people will be concerned about this issue. In fact, one of the primary rationales for taking sexual histories from the subject's point of view is that the interviewer is able to correct misinformation, to supply general and specific information when the subject requests it, and in all cases to present a nonjudgmental attitude that will at least relieve the subject's anxieties.

In interviewing people about their sex lives, there is one basic rule that governs the interviewer's behavior—*never make judgments about what people do or do not do.* This may seem self-evident, but it is sometimes disregarded and often is not as easy to remember as it appears to be. All of us have to some extent incorporated the cultural norms and attitudes about sex, most of them have become so deeply ingrained that they are not even recognized. Nevertheless, if the interviewer permits himself or herself to be influenced by these cultural impediments, the responses given by the subjects may be seriously affected.

Obviously, one of the best ways to overcome prejudices about what people do sexually is to become personally knowledgeable about every aspect of sexual behavior, but again, this is not so simple as it might appear. For example, it might be difficult for a heterosexual interviewer to get to know the homosexual world intimately by spending time in gay bars or parties unless he or she first confronts and substantially overcomes any lingering homophobic feelings. The same could be said for other varieties of sexual behavior such as prostitution and sadomasochism, activities about which few interviewers are likely to have much if any first-hand knowledge. It is undeniable, however, that the more we become personally acquainted with what goes on in the sexual world, the less likely we are to burden ourselves with prejudgments.

The problem is that we can't often hide our attitudes successfully. Respondents pick up clues from the interviewer's tone of voice, facial expressions, and body language. We know that a controlled, even manner of speaking, a pleasant expression, and a relaxed body posture best convey an attitude of acceptance to the person being interviewed, but it isn't easy for an interviewer to fake that appearance.

However, if the spirit of free inquiry is the basis of interviewing, it is plain that we can't impose our own standards, morals, and judgments in the process. If subjects are to be completely accessible the interviewer has to be neutral and accepting of other people's feelings and attitudes.

There can be no discrimination in this matter. The interviewer has to be as accepting of the rapist and the child molester as he or she is of the celibate. No one is to be judged. The interviewer's sole objective is to obtain information about all kinds of sexual behavior, completely excluding any prejudgments and prejudices.

The interviewer must avoid a quick answer to "Am I normal?" or "Is this particular behavior of mine normal?" It isn't that simple. For instance, suppose the subject wants to know if masturbation is normal. Certainly it is if we're talking about it from a statistical standpoint, since it is a virtually universal activity. Suppose a male subject reports that he masturbates by rubbing his penis against the bed. Since bed rubbing accounts for only about 5 percent of male masturbation, we would have to say that the masturbation is normal but the way that it is done is statistically infrequent and therefore "abnormal."

Similarly, any other kind of sexual behavior—homosexuality, oral sex, extramarital intercourse, and others—can be classified as either frequent or infrequent, normal or abnormal, statistically speaking. By that criterion, the common cold is normal because nearly everybody catches one. Clearly, then, frequency or infrequency does not constitute the best ground for deciding what is normal. The fallacy can best be seen by taking 50 percent as an arbitrary dividing line between what is common and what is not. By that measurement, male homosexuality is statistically normal because 50 percent of all males have either had an overtly homosexual experience or been aroused psychologically by other males. But female homosexuality would have to be considered statistically abnormal because only about 28 percent of females have had a homosexual experience or have been aroused psychologically by other females.

The law applies still another view of normality by classifying sexual acts as "natural" or "unnatural." Such behavior as anal intercourse, oral sex, and homosexuality are all cited as unnatural sex acts from the legal standpoint because they do not lead to procreation. These legal definitions, however, have little to do with actual sexual behavior.

In addition, "unnatural" literally means something that doesn't occur in nature or else runs counter to what is presumed to be human sexual nature. Even casual observation would tell us that animals sometimes engage in sex not just to procreate. Scientific investigation, in fact, shows that there is virtually nothing humans do sexually that isn't found in the animal world except perhaps transvestism, since animals of course don't cross-dress. In our society, having sex with young children is regarded as contrary to our sexual nature, but it occurs in other species and even in other human societies. Even forced sex has been observed among animals.

It is often argued that in the lower animals sexual intercourse occurs only for procreation because it takes place specifically during the time the female is ovulating and sexually receptive. This is a common misconception, easily disproved. For example, although intercourse occurs more often when the female is in heat, the female orangutang has intercourse throughout her pregnancy and, like the chimpanzee, also has it when she is not in heat.

There are those who argue that prostitution is unnatural because goods are exchanged for sexual favors. A female chimpanzee who is not in heat but is watching a male eat a banana will sometimes back up to him and present her genitalia for intercourse. If he is interested and begins to copulate with her, she turns around, grabs the banana, and runs.

Animal research also shows that two males or two females of the same species frequently have sex with each other, and that many animals masturbate themselves. In both cases, obviously, procreation is not involved. Moreover, sex play among young animals and between adults and the young is commonplace. This would lead us to conclude that a "natural" sex act is whatever people do sexually.

Thus far we have been talking about legal and scientific views of normality, but the overwhelming body of current attitudes on this subject can be traced to the Jewish laws established after the Jews left Babylonia and since incorporated in the so-called Judeo-Christian tradition. It is only within the past ten years or so that these laws have begun to change, through interpretation in some cases and through the writing of new laws in others. Such changes are slow, however, and the greatest movement toward a different set of attitudes is apparent in the churches themselves.

Many churches now minister to homosexual groups, without prejudice or attempts at conversion. Many Christian churches are not so concerned about premarital intercourse as they used to be, at least under some circumstances, and masturbation is now accepted by a large number of religious people as a universal phenomenon, even though they still don't talk about it openly. Nevertheless, the Judeo-Christian ethic, with its rigid views of sexual behavior and its numerous prohibitions, is still alive. There are many kinds of sexual behavior not sanctioned by organized religions which continue to exert a powerful influence on legislatures and other law-making and enforcing bodies, no matter how liberal individual members may be.

It isn't necessary to become pansexual to understand that the burden of sexual guilt that so many people carry can be awesome and terrifying. It is this guilt that expresses itself in the anxious question "Am I normal?" and "Is this normal?" In many cases, guilt can be directly traced to early religious training.

We continue to equate cleanliness and purity with "godliness" while sex is regarded as dirty and filthy. Genitals are unclean; people still think they have to wash their hands after urinating, although it is the hands that were dirty in the first place. Some men and women still regard menstruating women as "unclean," not to be touched, as they were considered in Biblical times. Similarly, people who think about sex "too much" (meaning more than the person making the judgment thinks about it) are also regarded as unclean.

Religion and the law are sometimes inconsistent about what they believe. For example, there is no law against masturbation in the United States unless it is done in public, and then the offense is "disturbing the peace" or "committing a public nuisance,'' not masturbation per se. Yet masturbation is considered a sin by the Catholic Church, and there is a heavy proscription against it among Orthodox Jews. Fundamentalist Protestants believe it is wrong, erroneously citing Onan casting his seed on the ground, but there is no church law against it. Since Protestant beliefs have largely determined the substance of our sex laws, no pressure has ever been put upon legislators to enact a law against masturbation. Still, Protestants generally tend to accept masturbation as something the young do, and many people try to prevent it by snatching the child's hand away from the genitals or saying it isn't proper behavior. Today many seem to regard masturbation as inevitable and acceptable if it is not done to ''excess,'' as defined by their own sexual activity.

It is generally assumed by these people, again erroneously, that people stop masturbating once they grow up, especially if they get married. Some of them sense or read that this isn't true, but publicly they do not change their attitudes.

In other aspects of sexuality, change moves slowly. Oral sex is prohibited by law in most states, although it is widely practiced. Cunnilingus and fellatio are classified in many states as unnatural sex acts, even within the context of marriage. Catholics, however, accept the behavior if it leads to intercourse and is not done ''for its own sake.'' But now nearly half the states have changed their laws about sex between consenting adults, so that oral sex, anal sex, and even homosexual behavior are no longer against the law if performed in private with mutual consent; this is not true, however, in about half the United States.

A rational view of ''normality'' and ''abnormality'' would be whether a particular kind of sexual activity is harming anyone else. Is masturbation harming anyone? Is extramarital intercourse harming someone? Is homosexuality? If rape occurs is anyone harmed? If an adult has sex with a young child, is harm done? This idea of harm or harmlessness perhaps comes closer to the idea of ''normal'' and ''abnormal'' behavior than any other definition. The definitive statement concerning normality is that there isn't anything that can be called ''normal'' or ''abnormal''; it is a meaningless concept. This idea needs to be understood by the interviewer and conveyed to the respondent.

3
Interviewing Techniques

It should be clear that the interviewer's objective is to elicit complete and accurate information from every subject. The most important way of ensuring this result is to maintain a nonjudgmental attitude, and several of the points discussed below concern ways of conveying the interviewer's lack of censure to the subject. Other techniques presented in this chapter have proved useful in encouraging the respondent to provide more detailed and explicit answers than he or she might otherwise give or to elicit more information than one might ordinarily get.

SETTING THE TONE OF THE INTERVIEW

It is a privilege to be allowed to take anyone's sexual history, and the respondent's willingness to share this material with an interviewer should be regarded as a sacred trust. One's sexual history is a very private affair. All the amenities showing respect and concern must be observed regardless of the social level or mentality of the respondent. Interviewers should be as concerned with the welfare and comfort of their subjects as they would be with those of a guest in their own homes.

The interviewer and respondent should be sitting *directly* facing each other, approximately 3½ to 4½ feet apart, on chairs or sofas of the same height. Anything that creates distance between interviewer and respondent should be avoided. One such distancing technique is to use a stilted and technical vocabulary. Another is to place a desk or table between interviewer and respondent. Another is to wear a white coat, which is a snobbish way of saying, "I am the professional and you are not."

The location of the interview, whether it is an office, an automobile, a living room, a bedroom, or even a bathroom, is not important as long as both people are comfortable. There must be absolute privacy so that no outsider can overhear.

Smoking tobacco should be freely permitted if the respondent smokes, as it often aids relaxation. On the other hand, if the respondent is offended by tobacco smoke the interviewer should refrain from smoking. Alcohol, marijuana, and other drugs often interfere with a person's ability to remember, perceive, and comprehend. If the subject is clearly under the influence of these substances, the interviewer would be well advised to postpone the interview.

ASSUME EVERYONE DOES EVERYTHING

A good technique in interviewing is to assume that everyone does almost everything, especially relatively common behaviors. Such an assumption does not mean that the interviewer believes that every subject has done everything, but rather that he or she is giving the respondent permission to report behaviors and experiences that are not generally revealed.

With this assumption in mind, questions are generally *not* phrased: "Do you masturbate?" or "Have you masturbated?" but rather, "How young were you when you first masturbated?" It is not helpful to assume that the subject has engaged in unusual or very rare behaviors. Questions about these less common behaviors are important to ask but should be phrased, "Have you ever . . .?" rather than "When was the first time . . .? or "How young were you . . .?"

If the interviewer is uncertain whether to assume that the subject has had a particular kind of experience, it is better to err in the direction of assuming the subject has had the behavior. For example, when inquiring about incest, the interviewer makes the assumption that the subject has had intercourse with a close relative almost without exception. The reason is that incest is so widely disapproved that the respondent is unlikely to report the experience unless he or she is made to feel that the interviewer is accepting of the behavior. The question would be asked in this form "Who is the closest relative with whom you have had any sexual contact?"

The decision whether or not to make an assumption depends on the particular history being taken and the interviewer's skill in identifying clues to atypical behaviors revealed in the interview. For instance, while interviewing a person who reports extensive sexual experience with a large number of different partners, the interviewer may make an assumption about prostitution and ask, "When were you first paid for intercourse?" By contrast, if the respondent is a moralistic and inhibited person who has given absolutely no clues to a wide and varied sexual life, the interviewer would make no assumption and would phrase the question "Have you ever been paid for intercourse?"

Such assumptions need to be made in nonsexual areas also. For example, when inquiring about drug use, it is better to ask, "How much pot do you smoke?" rather than "Have you ever tried marijuana?" Questions phrased in this manner give the respondent permission to say when the behavior began or to say that he or she never experienced marijuana smoking, whereas if the respondent is asked "Do you smoke grass?" he or she can quickly conceal the behavior behind a "no" response.

Respondents rarely answer in the affirmative if, indeed, they have not engaged in a particular behavior. If this does occur, asking for addditional details usually clears up the contradiction. For example, a person may admit to masturbation in an attempt to please the interviewer although he or she has never engaged in it. But the subsequent questions about frequencies and techniques will rapidly show the unfamiliarity with this behavior.

Some activities are common in certain social levels and groups and uncommon in others. As a result, the interviewer should be aware of typical differences in behavior among groups when deciding whether or not a particular question should be asked. One learns what is common at various social levels through contact with a wide variety of persons and through the literature.

POSITIVE FEEDBACK

As is illustrated throughout this book, the interviewer constantly gives positive feedback to the respondent by saying such things as "OK," "fine," "of course," "all right," "yes," "good," "I see," etc. At the same time the interviewer smiles, nods his or her head affirmatively while looking the respondent directly in the eye, and maintains an accepting body posture. When positive feedback is used for socially taboo behavior the message that is being conveyed is not "I approve of this behavior" but "I approve of your telling me this and I accept what you are telling me."

One day, one of the authors was approached by a troubled young man who had given his sex history more than a year earlier. The man said, "Remember me? I'm the homosexual, masochistic coprophile who gave you a history last year." The reply was "What is your problem—why are you troubled?" The man was amazed that his behavior was not regarded as his problem; his reaction to the behavior was.

OPENING AND CLOSING DOORS

The basic plan presented in this book, a systematic adherence to a predetermined outline, allows the interviewer a great deal of latitude in eliciting a wide range of information through direct questioning while enabling the interviewer to catch everything of significance.

A large part of every interview is concerned with getting areas of information or specific sexual behaviors identified. This skill is facilitated by a process called "opening and closing doors." In the interview process, one opens up directions, lines, or avenues of inquiry and closes those that do not require further exploration. To illustrate, if the interviewer asks, "When did you first have intercourse?" and the response is, "I've never had it," then, if the interviewer is satisfied with the response, it is not necessary to pursue the subject of intercourse further, and the interviewer closes that door.

A case of male impotence provides another good illustration. If a respondent mentions an impotence problem, it is important to find out what his level of alcohol consumption is. If it turns out to be very low or nonexistent, then alcohol can be eliminated as a contributing factor to the impotence. This door cannot be closed if the question is never asked.

Identifying areas of information through the "opening door" aspect of this process is illustrated by the following example concerning homosexuality. Either overt homosexual behavior or homophobia (fear that one might be homosexual) can be a very important factor in a person's life, whether or not there is a sexual dysfunction. If a question about homosexuality is never asked, the interviewer may never discover the individual's feeling about it, and this particular door may never be opened.

The opening and closing door process is clearly illustrated in the case history of a married man who has undergone eighteen years of psychotherapy with five different therapists. When asked in this interview how often he masturbated during his marriage, he revealed not only that he was doing it but, more importantly, that he was experiencing terrible guilt as a consequence and considered himself abnormal. Simply asking *how often* rather then *whether* he masturbated during the marriage opened the door that was of primary importance to his therapy. In eighteen years he had never divulged his masturbatory activity, apparently because he was never asked. Although he was perfectly willing to answer when the question was asked, through all those years and with five professionals, that particular door, a key to his therapy, had never been opened.

PEG SYSTEM

The purpose of interviewing is to establish a pattern, a mosaic, a picture, a history of the person being interviewed. There are specific items of general background information that are necessary to all interviews—for example, age, education, religion, occupation, family and parental background, avocations, medical history, etc. More specifically, the purpose of sex history interviewing is to identify an individual's sexual behavior, values, and attitudes. In addition to specific demographic information, the sex history covers a range of sexual behaviors.

Establishing the respondent's history is facilitated in the interview by the use of "pegs"—ways of relating items of information to significant events in the individual's life so as to increase the accuracy of the information being given. People's lives are filled with many "pegs" on which they hang events. Some examples are places where they lived, including different houses, cities, countries; their age at the time of important incidents or milestones such as high school graduation, college graduation, marriage, divorce, births of children, death of parents, religious rituals such as Bas or Bar Mitzvah or confirmation, surgery or serious illness, military service, etc. For example, "army brats" might identify their development of sexual behaviors and attitudes in relation to where the family was stationed at various significant points. Women in particular tend to peg events on their children's ages. Bar Mitzvahs or confirmations are especially important pegs because they occur at the critical age of puberty, at around thirteen years, when personal sexual awareness becomes acute.

One of the important early tasks in taking a sex history is to establish a whole series of these pegs appropriate to the individual being interviewed. This task is of prime importance to both the interviewer and the interviewee. For the interviewer, pegs provide a foundation or framework upon which a history can be built. In a practical sense, they are used as guides in soliciting information. For the interviewee, the pegs permit appropriate associations to be made to identify various kinds of information at specific intervals. For example, in determining the age at first coitus, the interview might proceed in this manner:

How old were you the first time you had intercourse?

I can't remember.

Can you remember what grade in school you were in?

I'm not sure.

Can you remember where you were living at the time?

Not really.

Was it before or after puberty?

Come to think about it, it was shortly after puberty. . . .

An additional benefit to the person being interviewed is that pegs are helpful in the development of one's own perceptions of one's sexual behavior. Divulging confidential information is difficult for many people. The process is more easily dealt with if the information can be put in a conceptual framework. Pegs set the foundation for that conceptualization and are instrumental in helping both the interviewer and the interviewee establish a pattern of the individual's life.

CHECKLISTS

It is very useful throughout the interview to have a series of checklists which can help the subject identify varieties of experiences, attitudes, and behaviors. The checklist system is a part of the structured component of the inventory. By identifying options, it facilitates the rapid pace of the interview. This system allows the interviewer to get additional information that might not be presented if the respondent is allowed to extemporize. Areas in the inventory in whch the checklist system is especially useful include petting techniques, coital positions, erotic fantasies, recreation, body image, and occupation of "johns" in the prostitution inventory. Each interviewer will no doubt identify other areas in which a checklist is helpful.

The following examples illustrate two ways in which the checklist system can be used:

a. *What do you do for recreation?*

   I love to ski.

   What else do you enjoy?

   I'm a sailboat enthusiast.

At this point, the interviewer is able to get at information not volunteered by the respondent by introducing a checklist of possible recreation activities.

Do you go to movies?

A little.

Go to dances?

No.

Watch TV?

Yes, a lot.

b. *How do you masturbate?*

With my hand mostly.

Do you also rub against bedding?

Sometimes.

Is there anal stimulation?

On occasion.

Do you use vibrators?

Most of the time.

Is there self-fellation?

I tried it two or three times, but no.

Over and above the use of checklists, one must explore additional behaviors when there is evidence that they exist. For example, if the masturbatory checklist is used and it is found that the respondent is familiar with many or most of the techniques listed, it is then necessary to spend several additional minutes exploring any unusual techniques that person may have used. If a person has a well-developed sadomasochistic history, this should be explored beyond the few questions that are routinely asked.

FOLLOWING THE LEAD OF THE RESPONDENT

In most cases the interview follows a fixed sequence of topics. There are, however, many occasions when the respondent takes the interviewer in a different direction. For example, a prostitute might be quite prepared to talk about her professional life but reluctant to talk about her personal life. In this case it would be a mistake to insist that she follow the designated order suggested in this book. It would be better to take her professional history first.

As another example, questions are asked about preadolescent sex play early in the sex history. If the respondent begins to tell about intercourse with her father at this point, the interviewer immediately alters the sequence of the interview in order to get the story of incest because the respondent has initiated the subject. If the interviewer does not take the respondent's lead, he or she may be giving the message that it is not proper to talk about this subject. The spontaneity of the situation will be lost and the information the respondent attempted to give the interviewer ignored.

It is important for the interviewer to develop the skill of sensing when to follow the lead of the respondent and when to return to the original sequence of items. For example:

What do you do for recreation?

I like to ski, but I haven't done it since my marriage broke up.

Since no questions have yet been asked about marriage, a productive continuation might be,

Oh, how long ago did your marriage break up?

Returning to the Recreation block *after* the response might be more appropriate.

Following the lead of the respondent can sometimes have humorous outcomes. An Armenian scientist with a rather heavy accent was giving a history. To the question, "How young were you when you first ejaculated?" he answered "14." The next question was, "And how did you ejaculate?" The answer was, "With a horse." Questions about sexual contact with animals are normally asked near the end of the history, but here, following the lead of the respondent, it seemed appropriate to ask about animal intercourse. The next question, therefore, was, "Fine. And back in Armenia, how often were you having intercourse with a horse?" At this point the respondent became embarrassed and reluctantly said, "Well, yes, I guess I did have intercourse with a pony then." After ages, frequencies, and techniques of his animal intercourse were elicited, it was discovered that what had sounded like "with a horse" was actually "with the whores." Fortunately no great harm was done in the interview, but a smoother history would have been taken if the interviewer had understood the respondent's remark for what it actually was.

AVOIDING EUPHEMISMS

The abundant use of euphemisms is a manifestation of the awkwardness felt by many people, both professional and nonprofessional, in discussing sexual behavior. For example, some common euphemisms for intercourse are: "having sex," "sleeping with somebody," "making love," "getting it on," "fooling around," "making out," "scoring," "going to bed."

Just as euphemisms for death (e.g., "passed on," "no longer with us") indicate a denial of death as a result of discomfort and a need to place distance between the event and conversation about it, so euphemisms for sexual behavior often function in the same way.

Euphemisms permit people to discuss sexual behavior in vague, ambiguous, indirect, relatively unintimidating ways. It is imperative that the professional not use euphemisms because doing so conveys to the listener the message that it is improper to talk about sexuality directly and that the topic must be talked around or softened for the sake of comfort.

It is equally important that the respondent not be allowed to use euphemisms, as this may reinforce the belief that it is not legitimate to discuss one's sexuality.

Euphemisms also prevent the interviewer and the respondent from reaching a clear agreement on exactly what is being discussed. For example, a response of "I slept with my wife three times last week" probably means that the man slept with his spouse seven nights and had intercourse three times.

There is a distinction between using words to avoid a direct reference to what is being discussed and using specialized words to facilitate communication. The next section on special vocabularies further spells out this difference.

SPECIAL VOCABULARIES

Too often clinicians (especially physicians) use a stilted vocabulary with their respondents. This creates distance between them rather than aiding communication. Even when the respondent understands what is being said, the fact that the scientific terms are often not part of his normal vocabulary means that their use is a subtle put-down. For example, a person at a lower social level understands the word "ill" but commonly uses the word "sick." Likewise, he or she understands the word "injured" but uses "hurt" instead. In both sexual and nonsexual matters, the vocabulary that the respondent is most accustomed to and comfortable with is the one to be used.

This becomes a learning process for the interviewer, who acquires the knowledge of what words to use primarily from the respondents. This holds particularly true when respondents differ from the interviewer in social level, age, racial group, and so forth.

The interviewer must be equally comfortable and relaxed using such words as "jacking off," "balls," "prick," "cunt," "shit," and "piss" as he is with "masturbation," "testicles," "penis," "vagina-vulva," "defecation," and "urination." Others have suggested that the interviewer should teach the interviewee "correct" words by gradually shifting from the vernacular to the scientific. We disagree. The word "balls" is just as "correct" as "testicles," and it is just as valid for the respondent to teach the interviewer how to talk "correctly." Using the vernacular word or phrase to express an idea is quite different from using a euphemistic word or phrase to mute or hide an idea.

It is also important for the interviewer to know, use, and be comfortable with the specalized argots used by certain groups. These specialized argots include both sexual and nonsexual words. In the prostitution argot, for example, a "john" is a customer and to "turn a trick" is to have intercourse for pay with a "john." In the homosexual argot, a "nellie" is an effeminate homosexual, and to "rim" is to have analingus. Just as the interviewer learns how to use different vocabularies from respondents, he or she also learns how to use specialized argots from the interview subjects. We have also urged elsewhere in this volume that it is desirable for the interviewer to know a wide variety of people on a personal or social level and that this can be an opportunity to learn different argots. Throughout this book we have given many examples in question-response sequences of different vocabularies and argots.

If the interviewer understands that a respondent's remark, such as "I love to cruise tearooms, but lace curtains through a glory hole make me sick," means "I love to have homosexual expeiences in public toilets but an uncircumcised penis inserted through a hole in the partitition repels me," the rapport between them would be immeasurably heightened. Rapport would similarly be increased if an interviewer correctly translated the following sentence spoken by a male prison inmate: "To cop a joint is worse than being a top and bottom man." Translation: to fellate a man is worse than having both active and passive anal intercourse.

A word of warning is in order. It is better not to use specialized argots than to use them incorrectly. The lower social level word "signify" used in some black cultures has many different subtle and regional nuances, and we would be hesitant to use it at the risk of affecting rapport adversely.

MULTIPLE QUESTIONS

Another technique of interviewing is to ask short, concise, single-purpose, direct rather than complex questions. For example, suppose a respondent had a horrible life with the father but loved the mother. If the interviewer asks a multiple question such as, "How did you get along with your father and mother?" the respondent will tend to recall the good relationship and repress the poor one and will report a wonderful relationship with the parents. It is more appropriate to ask separate questions: "How did you get along with your father?" and "How did you get along with your mother?"

The disadvantage of multiple questions is that people can ignore any part of the question they do not wish to answer and concentrate on the part they do want to answer. This is especially true in asking about sexual behavior. For example, when asked, "Do you have vaginal, oral, and anal sex?" the respondent can select the part of the question that is least intimidating to answer and may hope that the interviewer will not zero in on the unanswered parts.

Many media talk show hosts do a poor job of interviewing in that they ask multiple questions and hence never get the type of information they are really after. Multiple questions have the added disadvantages of confusing the respondent, giving the respondent an opportunity to take the interviewer on a long verbal "trip," and not allowing the interviewer to maintain control of the interview.

ANTICIPATING RESPONSES

One of the key techniques in successful interviewing is for the interviewer to anticipate an appropriate range of responses commensurate with the respondent's background and social level. There are, however, two aspects or concerns of which the interviewer needs to be aware. The first is to know what behavior, attitudes, and knowledge are typical of people of different social levels and different groups. The second is to be prepared for variations from the pattern.

To illustrate: in getting the history of a lower-class male, an interviewer can first anticipate that the respondent's history will be like that of other lower-class males; that is, the interviewer knows that the pattern of lower-class males includes relatively little masturbation later in life, experience with a large number of female partners, no particular interest in female erotic arousal or orgasmic response, etc.

On the other hand, the interviewer must recognize that not everyone falls into a stereotypical pattern and must be able to anticipate variations. Nudity, including sleeping nude and having intercourse nude, is not as readily acceptable at lower social levels as it is at upper levels. The interviewer must be alert to variations from this pattern when a person of a lower social level talks about nudity freely, experiences it openly, and exclaims that he or she enjoys it. Although the respondent is probably being honest about personal attitudes and experience, such a response is not typical of people at lower social levels.

Similarly, a male who says he has had intercourse with one hundred females but reports being aroused by thinking about females does not fall into an anticipated category, for the two sequences of experiences typically do not coincide. That is to say, the typical pattern of people who report high numbers of sexual partners is that they are so inundated with overt experience that they usually need more than psychological stimulation (thinking or seeing) to be aroused.

Part of the process of anticipating a range of responses is to be alert to answers that conflict with cultural patterns or sequences of experiences. Additional probing may well be necessary here to allay the interviewer's doubt.

SUGGESTING ANSWERS

The interviewer must avoid suggesting answers to the respondent. The following is an illustration of the wrong way to interview:

How often do you have intercourse with your wife?

Oh, I do that just about average—about the usual amount.

You mean about two or three times a week?

All the interviewer is doing is exposing his or her own coital frequency or personal ideas about average behavior.

Instead of responding with a specific frequency, the interviewer might suggest a range of answers in random order—that is, not in either an ascending or a descending sequence, but covering all possibilities. To illustrate the right way, the sequence might go:

How often do you have intercourse with your wife?

Oh, I do that just about average—about the usual amount.

Do you think it averages once a year, three times a day, once a month, five times a week?

Supplying a range of responses in no particular order gives the respondent a time frame to relate to, a frequency to relate to. The response might be:

Oh, it isn't as often as five times a week. But it's certainly more than twice a week.

In suggesting a range of possible answers, the interviewer includes some suggestions that go beyond any range that the respondent is likely to have. For example, if the range suggested is from once a day to once a year, and if the respondent averages more than once a day, he or she is more likely to reply "Once a day" rather than give the correct frequency.

RELIABILITY AND VALIDITY IN INTERVIEWING*

Reliability refers to the consistency and dependability of a given answer. For example, if a respondent in the first interview is asked, "How old were you when pubic hair first began to grow," and the answer is "10"; and in a second interview, the answer is "I think it was age 10 or 11" to the same question, that answer is reliable. On the other hand, if the answer is "age 10" in the first interview and "age 15" in a subsequent interview, the reliability of the response is low.

Validity refers to the truth of the answer. In the above example, even if the answer to the pubic hair question is highly reliable (on both occasions the respondent answered "age 10"), this is not proof that in *actuality* pubic hair began to grow at age 10. So in interviewing we are faced with two problems: (1) can the respondent accurately recall specific details of his or her sexual life, and (2) to what extent does the recollection reflect the reality of the respondent's life?

Reliability has been established for this sex history inventory with a minimum of two years and an average of four years between taking and retaking sex histories of the same people.

Validity is almost always more difficult to measure than reliability. In the example above, to measure validity the respondent would have to have observed and recorded when public hair growth began and then, years later, compare his or her recollection with the original observation. When such comparisons have been made, the responses have been virtually identical.

Several other ways of testing validity have been used. For example, the sex histories of a husband and wife should be the same in certain areas. For example, did they have intercourse with each other before marriage, what are their frequencies of marital intercourse, how long does it last, what positions are used, what are their petting techniques, how many abortions did the wife have in marriage? A high degree of validity has been found with all of these items.

There are also many clues that an interviewer receives while taking a sexual history which give indications of taboo overt behavior. For example, there are ten or twelve clues about homosexual behavior that are given before one asks the question, "How old were you the first time you had a homosexual experience?" If many of

*Based on research data reported in A.C. Kinsey, W.B. Pomeroy, and C.E. Martin, *Sexual Behavior in the Human Male* (Philadelphia: W.B. Saunders, 1948).

these clues are in a positive direction and the respondent nevertheless denies overt homosexual experience, he is confronted with the inconsistency and asked to explain it. In most cases, the respondent will then admit homosexual behavior or will be able to explain the inconsistency.

A sexual history can be falsified in three ways: exaggeration, misremembering, and cover-up. We have found that exaggeration is almost impossible to maintain because of the pace of the interview and because of the complexity and detail of the information sought. Persons who have deliberately tried to exaggerate have reported that it is almost impossible to accomplish. In addition, because of the nonjudgmental nature of the interview, there is little motivation to exaggerate. As indicated above, misremembering is minimal and is as often in one direction as the other.

It is most difficult for the interviewer to deal with cover-up. Establishing rapport, giving permission, and being alert to the many clues to overt behavior are the best ways to overcome this difficulty.

So far we have spoken about the reliability and validity of the subject's responses. But the interviewer must sometimes make subjective judgments, particularly when estimating the intensity of a respondent's feeling. In taking histories at the Kinsey Institute, occasionally the interviewers cross-checked to determine how accurate their judgments were by sitting in on one another's history taking and recording independently. The judgments were found to be about 98 percent reliable, suggesting that familiarity with the technique gives the interviewer increasing confidence in his ability to interpret responses correctly.

COMMANDING THE INTERVIEW

One of the most difficult techniques for an interviewer to learn is how to take charge of and maintain the rapid pace of the interview. If the interviewer is interested in gathering information from the respondent, the basic attitude should be "Come hell or high water, I need certain information from you, and by God I'm going to get it!" This is quite different from the usual attitude that "the customer is always right," or "how can I protect the respondent from psychological onslaught, including my own?" The interviewer must be in the driver's seat and must be fully in command, directing and controlling the interview. This does not mean that he or she should be insensitive to the respondent or disregard his or her emotional state. There are times in the interview when the respondent is perceived to be emotionally upset over a particular part of the history, and if this occurs the interviewer will do well to abandon this line of questioning and move on to a less traumatic topic or area. When this occurs, however, the interviewer needs to return to the emotionally upsetting part of the history later, when he or she judges that the respondent is capable of dealing with it.

The interviewer also needs to determine when an interruption or a change of topic is indicated. Not infrequently, respondents tell long, detailed stories (in the vernacular, this is called "being taken on a trip"). Sometimes these so-called trips are very important in giving insight into the respondent's life but often they are means of avoiding the specific sexual history. The interviewer needs to decide which of these categories the "trip" falls into and whether he or she should interrupt the "trip" or let it continue.

We believe that the trip should be interrupted in the majority of cases because at this stage in the contact with the respondent an overall framework of his or her life is necessary without filling in the details. "Trips" can best come later after the framework is established.

Development of skills in using these techniques enables one to get accurate, complete information.

FIGURE 4-1

BACKGROUND INFORMATION

HEALTH			DREAMS		INCIDENTAL PROSTITUTION	
		PRE-ADOLESCENT SEX PLAY		PREMARITAL COITAL ATTITUDES	EXTRA-MARITAL COITUS	CONTRACEPTION
	EROTIC AROUSAL					
MARRIAGE			PREMARITAL PETTING	FIRST COITUS		INCIDENTAL HOMOSEXUALITY
		PUBERTY				
	FAMILY BACKGROUND				MARITAL COITUS	ANIMAL CONTACTS
ANATOMY		SELF MASTURBATION	RECREATION	PREMARITAL COITUS		OTHER SEXUAL BEHAVIORS
	SEX EDUCATION					
			GROUP SEX			

4
Coding and Recording

The code for recording information developed by Dr. Alfred Kinsey is what is known as a position code. The meaning is derived from the position of the symbols on the page as well as from the symbols themselves. For example, a check mark ✓ at one place on the page will mean "Yes, I like to cook," while in another position on the page the same symbol will stand for "I learned about masturbation by being told about it." A **14** in one position will mean "I had my first menstrual period at age 14," and at another place it will mean "I've had two years of college."

The code was designed with two features in mind: first that it would be virtually impossible to break, thus ensuring the confidentiality of the material, and second that it would be compact and therefore easy to use and economical to file. The *Kinsey Reports* are proof that an enormous mass of data can be recorded securely in a relatively brief time, requiring little storage space and few materials. The code is secure, economical, and, once learned, easy and quick to use. Minor modifications of the coding by each interviewer will ensure confidentiality.

Dr. Kinsey's code evolved from his early laboratory work with gall wasps, when he was using twenty-eight different measurements to record color and length of wings, size, and other characteristics. He was dismayed by the tedium of the task since there were millions of gall wasps to record, so he devised a brief shorthand system. When he became interested in taking sexual histories, he quite naturally adapted this code.

Soon after Kinsey became interested in studying human sexuality, he devised a brief questionnaire which he handed out to graduate students in biology. One question he asked of the male students was, "Are your testes descended?" To his surprise, a majority of the responses stated that only one was descended. He knew this couldn't be true, because undescended testes are uncommon; consequently he discussed this question with his students and soon realized that they had misinterpreted it to mean, ''Does one testis hang lower than the other?''

At that point, Kinsey abandoned the questionnaire and began to ask questions of his subjects directly. Believing that note taking during the questioning would interfere with his rapport with the subjects, he tried to commit the entire interview to memory and would rush to another room after it was over and write down everything he could recall. But this method was obviously inefficient and time-consuming; besides, data were lost because total recall was impossible. Thus he was forced into recording. As he began to code the material, he found that he was able to maintain his rapport with people and that the interview and coding moved along at a fluid pace.

Eighty percent of the questions on the history were developed within two weeks and the remaining 20 percent during the next six months.

The interview is recorded on a prepared form on a standard 8½ ʺ by 11 ʺ sheet, easily filed or slipped into a notebook. The paper should be of high rag quality so that it will not yellow or become brittle with age. It is best to write with a fine-point pen because the coding is written in a very small area, with the marks close together; the pen will not smudge as a pencil would. It is advisable to print rather than to use cursive writing, and some practice may be needed to improve one's legibility.

The recording sheet is composed of 24 well-defined blocks which contain a varied number of spaces. As noted, the meaning of a symbol depends upon its position within a particular block. The 24 specific aspects of the sexual history recorded in the blocks are as follows (identified by their chapter number in this book):

5. Background Information	17. Premarital Intercourse
6. Health	18. Incidental Prostitution
7. Recreation	19. Premarital Coital Attitudes
8. Family Background	20. Marital Coitus
9. Marriage	21. Extramarital Coitus
10. Sex Education	22. Contraception
11. Puberty	23. Erotic Arousal
12. Preadolescent Sex Play	24. Anatomy
13. Self-Masturbation	25. Group Sex
14. Dreams	26. Incidental Homosexuality
15. Premarital Petting	27. Animal Contacts
16. First Coitus	28. Other Sexual Behaviors

Figure 4–1 shows the arrangement of these 24 blocks on the recording sheet.

There is sufficient space on the bottom of the recording sheet for expanding, adding, or exploring replies. An asterisk is used to indicate when a response is continued at the bottom of the sheet. Remarks recorded in the space below the blocks are written in an abbreviated style—that is, vowels are omitted and only the consonants are used to represent the word, along with common symbols. In this way, ideas can be recorded in a very limited space.

Example of code in abbreviated style:

Marr. bd bcs ♂ alcol + Cx

Translation: The marriage is bad because the husband abuses alcohol and has extra-marital intercourse.

The code is flexible enough to record a vast spectrum of human behavior, the usual and the unusual, the anticipated and the extraordinary.

As the following glossary indicates, the code is comprised of mathematical signs, numbers, letters, and other simple symbols. Because it is the position of a symbol in the block that indicates its meaning, relatively few symbols can be used. For example, in the Family Background block, **M** stands for mother; where marital status is noted, **M** represents marriage; **M** also symbolizes masturbation; in the religion block **M** may be used to indicate that the respondent is a Methodist; and in addition, **M** is the symbol for masochist.

The code below presents the most commonly used symbols and abbreviations. Special symbols used for certain blocks are indicated in the appropriate chapter.

COMMON ABBREVIATIONS

a	active example; e.g., **GOa** means respondent is the active participant in genital-oral activity rather than the passive receiver, **GOp**
Ab	induced abortion
A	aunt; approval (in Homosexual block)
B	Baptist; black; books
BS	bisexual
BD	Bull-dyke
C	Catholic; confirmation; coitus; companion; city
Cpm	premarital coitus
Cm	marital coitus
Cx	extramarital coitus
Cd	coitus after break-up of marriage
cf	refer to
CL	common law: lived openly as husband and wife for at least a year; does not apply to homosexual community
cli	climax; orgasm
cos	cousin
-d	to date
D	dreams; disapprove (only in Homosexual block)
d	day
Div	divorced
Die	died

e	each
f	formerly
F	father
G	genitalia
GC	gonorrhea
gd	grade down; diminishing in frequency
gu	grade up; increasing in frequency
GO	genital-oral
H	homosexual
HS	public high school
Hsb	husband
J.	Jewish
kp	keep
li	lower inhibitions
M	marriage; mother; Methodist; masturbation; masochist
Mil	military
m	minutes; mutual; month
O	does not apply. Example: If a person has had no extramarital coitus all the questions in the block would be recorded O
P	puberty; peers; petting; Protestant
p	passive
Pa	adult (only used in Sex Education block)
PS	private high school; psychiatrist
Ψ	psychologist
Pr	prostitute
R	rural; religion
ref	referral
sib	siblings
Sep	separated
S	sadist; single
Sp	spontaneous abortion
T	teacher
th	thought about (only in Masturbation block)
TV	transvestite
TS	transsexual

U	urban; uncle
V	virgin
W	white
Wf	wife
w	with; week
ww	without
y	year
Z	zoophilia

SIGNS AND SYMBOLS

♀	female
♂	male
✓	always; yes; many; very; regularly
±	somewhat; now and then; less than a ✓
−	infrequently; rarely; occasionally
X	no; never; not; nothing; complete negative
✓ ✓	extreme positive response
✓ ✓ ✓	alcoholic; excessive; abusive
XX	extreme negative response
→	passage of time; progression from one point in time to another
-	up until or through
( )	age before adolescence; also used to set a reply apart. For example, ✓-10 may mean ± at 10 but ✓ (10) means a check up to age 10.
" "	what the respondent says, implying that the interviewer did not believe what was said.
[ ]	what the interviewer believes. For example, if a respondent says moral reasons are not a factor in refraining from premarital intercourse but the interviewer is skeptical, the proper coding would be "X" [✓].
◯	a circle is placed around the age a deceased person would have reached at the time of history taking, followed by age of respondent when the death occurred. Example: ⑮ 9 Bro means the respondent's brother would be 15 years old if he had lived, but he died when the subject was 9.
*	remarks continued at bottom of the page
!	true and unusual

A four-symbol system is used to code degrees of frequency. A checkmark, ✓, means yes, positive, affirmative, of course, or always, depending on the context. An **X** means no, never, negative. A minus sign, −, denotes a small amount, rare, unusual, infrequent. A plus-or-minus sign, ±, stands for somewhat, more or less, or not always. For example, in coding the amount of alcohol consumption:

X	no alcohol at all
−	an occasional social drink
±	a few drinks a week and/or getting high on rare occasions
✓	1–3 drinks a day
✓ ✓	more than 8 oz. of alcohol a day
✓ ✓ ✓	alcoholic

Combinations of these symbols are also used. For instance, something that falls between a check and a plus-or-minus is called a check plus-or-minus ✓ ±. Something so rare that it is almost nonexistent but nevertheless is still mentioned might be recorded as − **X**. These and other variants are illustrated in the chapters on the individual blocks.

When age, frequency, or date is sought, the numbers themselves are often used. If the respondent was 25 years old at the time a certain behavior took place or if he is 5′11″ in height, the actual number, **25** or **5′11″**, is inserted on the form.

It is possible to go beyond the scale. For example, if someone not only does not drink alcohol but belongs to the Women's Christian Temperance Union, he or she could be given an **XX** to emphasize the fact that the response is a very strong negative.

The check system is subjective because the interviewer must very often guess the intensity of the respondent's feeling. For example, if the interviewer asks, "Do you like to cook?" and the respondent replies, "Yes, I like to cook," that might warrant a check, but if the answer is, "Well, yes, I guess I like to cook," that response isn't nearly so enthusiastic and should be recorded as a ±.

It is most important for the interviewer to have his own set of definitions, and to adhere to them consistently. For example, in the coding for alcohol consumptions shown above, different interviewers might use different criteria for light or heavy use.

The code is in part based on degree. For example, a percentage figure is recorded when a prostitute is asked, "What percent of your tricks return to you more than once?" or when the interviewee is asked, "What percent of time do you climax?"

Distributions of frequency are recorded by indicating the number of times above the slash mark, /, and whether the standard is by day, week, month, or year below the slash. If it's by the week, the **w** is not used, since most people seem to think in terms of weeks.

For example:

4 times a week is recorded **4/**
4 times a day is recorded **4/d**
4 times a month is recorded **4/m** or **1/**
4 times a year is recorded **4/y**

3 to 4 times a week is recorded **3-4/**
once a month can be coded as either **1/m** or **1/4** (once every 4 weeks)

Since the interviewer is often obliged to do some mental arithmetic in order to record simply and economically, calculations are made on the basis of a fifty-week year. If something happened six times a year, therefore, it could be recorded as **6/y** or **1/8.**

A numerical attitude scale from **1** to **4** is used to measure degrees. For example, degrees of marital happiness are recorded as follows:

1 very happy
2 more happy than unhappy
3 more unhappy than happy
4 very unhappy

A coding of **1→4** means that the marriage began as very happy and changed to very unhappy. A relationship recorded as **2-3** means that it is sometimes more happy than unhappy, and at other times more unhappy than happy.

When the interview is over, the interviewer quickly scans his coded sheet to check whether there are any blanks indicating that a question was not asked. Before the respondent leaves, the interviewer can easily ask these questions to ensure that a complete history has been taken.

BACKGROUND INFORMATION					
HEALTH			DREAMS		INCIDENTAL
					PROSTITUTION
				PREMARITAL	CONTRACEPTION
		PRE-		COITAL	
		ADOLESCENT		ATTITUDES	EXTRA-
	EROTIC	SEX PLAY			MARITAL
	AROUSAL				COITUS
MARRIAGE					
		PREMARITAL	FIRST		INCIDENTAL
		PETTING	COITUS		HOMOSEXUALITY
		PUBERTY			
				MARITAL	ANIMAL
	FAMILY			COITUS	CONTACTS
	BACKGROUND				
ANATOMY				PREMARITAL	
		SELF-	RECREATION	COITUS	
		MASTURBATION			OTHER
					SEXUAL
					BEHAVIORS
	SEX				
	EDUCATION				
			GROUP SEX		

FIGURE 5-1

5

Background Information

When taking a history, certain key pieces of information are needed immediately. For example, age and marital status are related to many aspects of sexual behavior and are primary references throughout the interview. These and other pieces of demographic information are placed at the top of the recording form for ready reference.

FIGURE 5-2

5 6	7 11	4	8	3	2	1
9 10		12 13				

Figure 5-1 shows the location of the Background block in relation to the other blocks (it occupies the two top sections running across the width of the recording sheet). Figure 5-2 shows where the responses to the thirteen background items are recorded on the form. The numbers, of course, do not appear on the actual recording sheet. The blank spaces on the second line can be used to record the respondent's occupational and educational history, if it is especially detailed. The space below the form can be used to elaborate on any information that will not fit into the prescribed space.

The thirteen items that make up this block are as follows:

1. Code number
2. Sex
3. Date of interview
4. Referral source and name
5. Age
6. Birth date
7. Marital status

8. Relationship to other respondents
9. Race
10. Religion and degree of observance
11. Current and former places of residence
12. Current and former occupations
13. Years of education

Figure 5–3 shows how a typical background information block is filled in.

FIGURE 5-3

21		*S*		*Frnd·Jhn Wsn* X						*10-12-79*	*♂*	*15*
	12-6-58		LA NYC									
W PXf v (-14) B			NY-13 CA-2	Sfclrk@ 20 15 UCLA ⩒		—		—				

The first three items are not, strictly speaking, questions since they can generally be supplied in advance of the interview.

Item 1

A code number is assigned to each respondent to ensure the confidentiality of the information supplied. The respondent's name, address, telephone number, and code number are kept in a separate file. Code numbers are generally assigned consecutively, but on occasion a more complicated code may be used—for example, to identify the interviewer. In Figure 5–3, the record indicates that this is the fifteenth interview in the series.

Item 2

The sex of the respondent is recorded using either the male, ♂, or the female, ♀, symbol. The interviewer usually knows the subject's sex before the interview from his or her name or from a telephone conversation, and can record it in advance, but there may be cases in which the sex of the respondent is not known until the person is actually seated in front of the interviewer—for example, if he or she has an ambiguous name and an unusually deep or high-pitched voice. In even rarer cases—for example, if the respondent is a transsexual—the interviewer may have to ask. In Figure 5-3, the record indicates that the subject is male. If the subject claims to be a male-to-female transsexual, that datum would be recorded as " ♀ " with quotation marks to indicate that the respondent identified him or herself in this manner.

Item 3

Obviously the date of the interview can be recorded in advance. In Figure 5-3, the record indicates that it took place on October 12, 1979.

Question 4

Who referred you?

A friend.

The name of your friend?

John Wilson.

Question 4 elicits the occupation of the person who sent the respondent for the interview (physician, psychiatrist, minister) or his or her relationship to the respondent (lawyer, friend, aunt, brother). Next to this information, the actual name of the referral agent is recorded in abbreviated writing, for confidentiality as well as efficiency. This information is sometimes known before the interview begins. It is rarely important unless it is necessary to go back to the referral source to cross-check information or for consultation (in the case of patients in therapy).

Question 5

How old are you?

21.

Question 6

When were you born?

December 6, 1958.

Questions 5 and 6 are both asked because it has been found that people at lower social levels tend to give their age at *next* or nearest birthday when asked "how old are you," whereas people at higher social levels more often give age at last birthday.

This is a good example of the interviewer's constant obligation to do mental arithmetic, as will be clear in later chapters.

Question 7

Are you single or married?

Single.

Marital status has three possible answers. If the person has never been married, the symbol **S** is used for single. If he or she is currently married, the symbol **M** is used. If he or she has been married in the past but is now divorced or widowed, the symbol **D** is used. In this interview we do not differentiate among divorced, widowed, or separated people because our interest is in the social aspects of the history—one's status in society. By this criterion, a person is married, never married, or previously but no longer married; these are the only three categories that concern us here.

Item 8

This item is a cross-reference to any relative or sexual partner of the respondent from whom the interviewer has a history. In most cases the subject may not even know whether or not any relative or sexual partner has been interviewed. The interviewer usually knows the answer in advance and records it without asking the question. If there is a cross-reference, the recording might be, for example, **bro 106**, indicating the relationship—in this case brother—and the case number of the previous interview. Figure 5–3 shows that neither the subject nor the interviewer knew of any relationship between the subject and a previous respondent.

Question 9

The race of the subject may be clearly revealed by the color of his or her skin. If it is not, or if the interviewer does not wish to rely on observation, he or she asks:

What is your race?

White.

Race is decided by social identification—how the person is perceived in society. If the person is regarded as black, then he is socially black, and that is what his social status is. If he passes as white although his parentage is black (or Oriental, Indian, etc.) he would be considered white because socially he is white. These are suggestions. Race may be defined and recorded to suit the objectives of the interviewer. In some cases ethnicity is the important issue.

Question 10

What is your current religion?

Baptist.

The three major religions are recorded as follows: Catholic, **C**; Protestant, **P**; Jewish, **J**. Any others are recorded in speedwriting. If the response is that the individual has no religion, it is recorded as **X**.

The check system is used to record the frequency of church attendance.

How often do you attend church?

I don't go at all now, but I did go regularly until I was 14 years old.

Thus, in Figure 5–3, **PXf⁄(-14)** indicates that the respondent is Protestant, **P**, no longer attends church at all, **X**, but did so frequently, **f** = formerly, **⁄** = very, until he was 14. If the interviewer decides the information is important, he may record **B** for "Baptist" at the far right line of Question 10.

Question 11

Where were you born?

I was born in New York City.

Where did you live after that?

I lived in New York until I was 13, and then moved to California. I now live in Los Angeles.

The cities in which the respondent has lived for at least a year are recorded chronologically in abbreviated form above the line. The city of birth is first with the others above it in sequence. Below the line, the states or countries in which the respondent has lived are listed chronologically with the state or country of birth first and the others below it. If extra space is needed, the interviewer supplies an asterisk and completes the information at the bottom of the page.

Question 12

What is your occupation?

I'm a student.

Have you held any jobs?

Yes, I was a clerk for a year when I was 20.

Question 13

How far did you get in school?

I'm a junior in college.

This is recorded as **15** because a college junior has had fifteen years of formal schooling.

What college do you go to?

UCLA.

What is your major?

Psychology.

Psychology is recorded as ψ because this is the Greek letter *psi*, customarily used for that discipline. In other instances, speedwriting is used.

Special coding for education is as follows:

All grades below the twelfth are coded by indicating the last grade the subject *started*

12	twelfth grade or high school graduate
12 +	more than high school but not college (i.e., vocational/technical school)
13	at least started first year of college
14	at least started second year of college
15	at least started third year of college
16	at least started fourth year of college
17	at least started graduate study
18	M.S., M.A., M.S.W., LLB., etc; in other words, eighteen years of schooling
19	**A.B.D.** indicates a Ph.D. candidate who has completed all the requirements except the dissertation
20	M.D., Ph.D., indicating twenty years of schooling

BACKGROUND INFORMATION						
HEALTH			DREAMS		INCIDENTAL PROSTITUTION	
		PRE-ADOLESCENT SEX PLAY		PREMARITAL COITAL ATTITUDES	EXTRA-MARITAL COITUS	CONTRACEPTION
	EROTIC AROUSAL					
MARRIAGE			PREMARITAL PETTING	FIRST COITUS		INCIDENTAL HOMOSEXUALITY
		PUBERTY				
	FAMILY BACKGROUND				MARITAL COITUS	ANIMAL CONTACTS
ANATOMY		SELF-MASTURBATION	RECREATION	PREMARITAL COITUS		OTHER SEXUAL BEHAVIORS
	SEX EDUCATION		GROUP SEX			

FIGURE 6-1

6
Health

For most subjects, answering the questions in the Health block is not a problem. For those who have medical problems, of course, it will take longer and may arouse some anxieties.

The respondent is first asked to evaluate his or her current health, meaning health since puberty, or from about age 13 to the present. Questions about health during childhood (from birth through age 12) cover congenital defects, illnesses, surgery, accidents, and other incidents. We are especially interested in knowing whether ill health may have interfered with the socialization process when the subject was a child. For example, a birth defect, a missing limb, cancer, serious burns, disfiguring surgery, or similar problems may have influenced the subject's social development. Also of interest is whether the illness kept the person out of school for as long as a year or more, thus having a direct effect on socialization. Individual researchers and therapists may wish to expand the Health block for their own purposes.

Disabled persons, especially disabled children, are often regarded as asexual in our culture. This cultural attitude and the policies it fosters have seriously retarded the social-sexual development of many sick and disabled persons.

There are persons who are disabled from an objective point of view—for example, the blind or people who bear serious scars—who do not consider themselves handicapped. In such cases the interviewer records the disability, indicating the disparity between his or her observation and the subject's self-report.

CODING FOR HEALTH QUESTIONS

✔   good health

±   fair health

   −   poor health

X   very poor health, or near death

If a subject reports excellent health but has an obvious physical or mental disability, what is said is recorded in quotes, " ", and what is perceived is recorded in brackets, [ ]. A hypochondriac would be recorded " − ", and the interviewer's observation ✓. Clues to the subject's attitudes toward health will be picked up in this block, because the questions are open ended. Speedwriting or other abbreviations are used extensively here to record specific health problems. For example, [amp] indicates the interviewer's observation that the subject has had an amputation to which he or she did not refer when asked about health. This information is placed within the block or at the bottom of the form.

The Health block, shown in Figure 6–1, is divided vertically so that responses are recorded for the current period on the left and for childhood on the right. Six spaces are provided so that responses can be recorded in as much detail as necessary. (See Figure 6–2.)

If the subject responds positively for either or both time periods when asked to evaluate his or her health, no further questions need be asked unless the interviewer is particularly interested in health as a factor in the subject's social and sexual life. If that is the case, the interviewer may decide to ask about medication and perhaps a checklist of illnesses.

Figure 6–3 shows how a typical interview on health might be recorded.

FIGURE 6-2

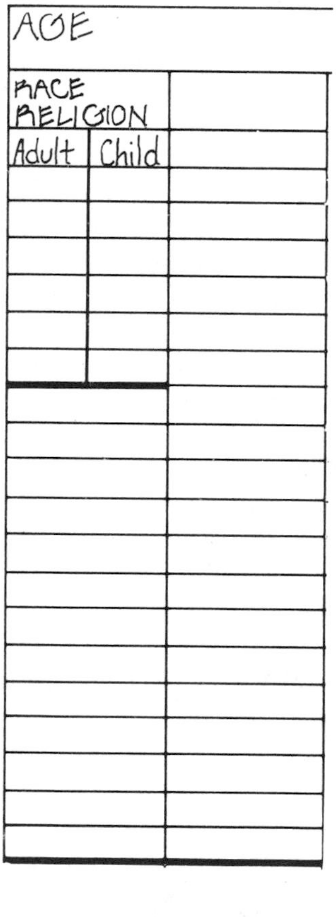

FIGURE 6-3

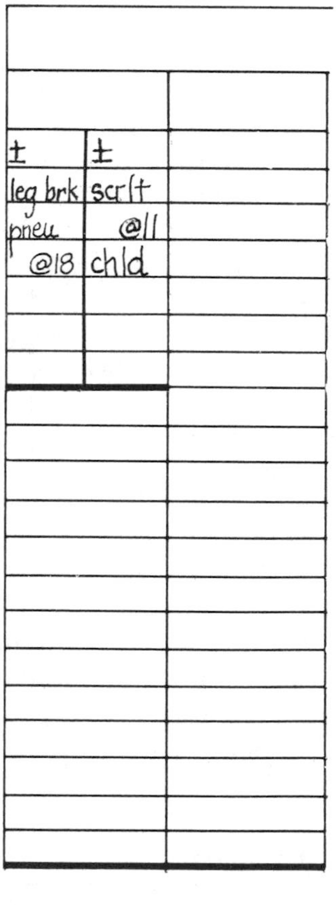

Question 1

Are you in good health now?

or

Are you sick now?

or

What medicine are you taking at the present time?

or

Are you currently in good health?

Oh, I guess so.

What makes you doubtful?

Well, I broke my leg last year and it's still not back to normal.

Have you had any serious illness as an adult?

Yes, I had pneumonia.

How old were you?

18.

Anything else you can remember?

Other than flu and colds, no.

O.K.

Question 2

Were you in good health as a child?

or

When you were young, were you sick often?

Oh, no, I had measles, mumps, chicken pox, and lots of earaches, from swimming.

Yes, but did you have any illnesses that kept you out of school for a long period of time, about a year or more?

Yes. I had to repeat the seventh grade when I had scarlet fever.

You were about 11?

Yes.

Was there anything else, any accidents, surgery, or other illnesses, during childhood?

Not that I can remember.

BACKGROUND INFORMATION

HEALTH

DREAMS

INCIDENTAL
PROSTITUTION

PREMARITAL
COITAL
ATTITUDES

CONTRACEPTION

PRE-
ADOLESCENT
SEX PLAY

EXTRA-
MARITAL
COITUS

EROTIC
AROUSAL

MARRIAGE

PREMARITAL
PETTING

FIRST
COITUS

INCIDENTAL
HOMOSEXUALITY

PUBERTY

MARITAL
COITUS

ANIMAL
CONTACTS

FAMILY
BACKGROUND

ANATOMY

SELF-
MASTURBATION

RECREATION

PREMARITAL
COITUS

OTHER
SEXUAL
BEHAVIORS

SEX
EDUCATION

GROUP SEX

FIGURE 7-1

7
Recreation

Recreation is defined here as nonsexual behavior which generally is easy to discuss. Questions about recreation are therefore valuable as an ice-breaker and come early in the interview. They reveal a good deal about lifestyles. If the subject replies that sex is his or her recreation, the interviewer says, ''We will come to that.''

We have suggested fifteen specific areas of exploration, but if the respondent mentions a particular hobby or major interest that is not on the checklist, it can be recorded in abbreviated form on the three blank lines at the bottom of the block.

What do you do for recreation (or for fun or for pleasure)?

I guess I like to fix up old cars. Recorded as **fx crs**
I play chess. **chess**

It is important to accept the subject's statements about his or her hobbies, but the interviewer also needs to go through the entire checklist because it contains the most popular kinds of recreation.

Figure 7–1 shows the location of the Recreation block in relation to other blocks. The location of the responses is shown in Figure 7–2. The checklist of activities is as follows:

1. Movies
2. Social dancing
3. Cards
4. Gambling
5. Reading
6. Television
7. Music
8. Sports

9. Housework
10. Sewing
11. Cooking
12. Cigarette, pipe, or cigar smoking

13. Drinking
14. Marijuana
15. Other drugs

The degree to which the respondent pursues these activities is recorded using the following code:

✓✓   more than once a week

✓   once a week

±   once a month

–   2 or 3 times a year

X   never

Figure 7–3 shows a coded version of a Recreation inventory.

FIGURE 7-2

	1 2	
	3 4	
	5 6	
	7 8	
	9 10	
	11 12	
	13 14	
	15	

FIGURE 7-3

	✓ –	
	± ✓	
	✓ ±	
	✓✓ LSD 1x	
	Bd trp	
	– ✓	
	± ✓✓	
	X ✓	
	✓✓	

Question 1

How often do you go to the movies?

Once a week. ✓

Question 2

How often do you go dancing?

Maybe once or twice a year. −

Question 3

How often do you play cards?

We have a group that meets once a month. ±

Question 4

How often do you gamble?

I am at the track every day. ✔ ✔

Are the stakes high enough to hurt you?

Yes.

It would be necessary here to find out if the subject is suffering financially because of gambling. A ✔ ✔ indicates that gambling has a major adverse effect on the subject's life.

Question 5

How much recreational reading do you do?
This is reading for recreation. Graduate students who read for their work or doctors who read all the time to keep up professionally would not be considered recreational readers.

I read about a book a week. ✔

I read a book every three or four months plus the newspaper. ±

I read the newspaper and *Newsweek*. −

I don't read much—maybe a sports magazine now and then. −

Question 6

How much television do you watch?

About three hours a day. ✔

CODING SYSTEM

✓ ✓	more than 3 hours a day
✓	3 hours a day
±	up to 2–3 hours/day
–	rarely; special event
X	never

Question 7

How often do you listen to music?

In the car—about an hour a day. ✓**p**

Do you play an instrument?

Yes, the piano. ✓**a**

This question is concerned with active and passive interest in music, indicated by **a** and **p** respectively.

Question 8

How often do you attend or watch sporting events?

I watch at least a game a week. ✓**p**

Do you participate in sports?

Yes, I play tennis three times a week. ✓**a**

Up to this point we've been interested in what people do, not what they would like to do. People who say that they love to go to the movies but are very busy and can't go more than a couple of times a year still rate a minus.

The next three questions—9, 10, and 11—are concerned with what the respondents *like* to do rather than what they actually do. (A cultural note: many men like to cook; many women do not. There may be clues here for homosexual or transsexual behavior, but one must be careful not to make judgments.)

Question 9

Do you like to do housework?

No. **X**

Question 10

Do you like to sew?

Yes. ✔

Question 11

Do you like to cook?

Yes, very much. ✔ ✔

Question 12

How much do you smoke cigarettes, pipe, cigars?

A pack of cigarettes a day. ✔

CODING SYSTEM

✔ ✔	2 packs a day, etc.
✔	a pack a day
±	2 packs a week
X	not at all

Frequency of pipe smoking is measured by the number of times a day the bowl is filled. The actual number of cigars smoked daily is recorded.

Question 13

How often do you take a drink?

I have one every night before dinner! ±

CODING SYSTEM

X	no alcohol at all
—	an occasional social drink
±	a few drinks a week and/or getting high on rare occasions
✔	1–3 drinks a day
✔ ✔	more than 8 oz. of alcohol a day
✔ ✔ ✔	alcoholic

Question 14

How often do you smoke marijuana?

I share a joint several times a week with friends. ✓

CODING SYSTEM

✓ ✓	pot head—every day
✓	several times a week
±	occasionally
−	very infrequently—2 or 3 times a year
X	never

Question 15

How often do you take other drugs?

I took LSD once at a party.

What happened?

I was sick and had a bad trip. **Ill-bd trip**

    Here is a checklist of popular street drugs:

Cocaine
Heroin
LSD
Amphetamines
Barbiturates

    If a person has an extensive drug history, one must use an asterisk and go to the bottom of the page.

BACKGROUND INFORMATION

HEALTH

DREAMS

INCIDENTAL
PROSTITUTION

PREMARITAL

PRE-

COITAL

CONTRACEPTION

ADOLESCENT

ATTITUDES

EXTRA-

EROTIC

SEX PLAY

MARITAL

AROUSAL

COITUS

MARRIAGE

PREMARITAL

FIRST

INCIDENTAL

PETTING

COITUS

HOMOSEXUALITY

PUBERTY

MARITAL

ANIMAL

FAMILY

COITUS

CONTACTS

BACKGROUND

ANATOMY

PREMARITAL

SELF-

RECREATION

COITUS

MASTURBATION

OTHER

SEXUAL

BEHAVIORS

SEX

EDUCATION

GROUP SEX

FIGURE 8-1

8

Family Background

The Family Background block is quite small for the large amount of material that is recorded within it, illustrating the exceptionally expeditious use of confined space in the inventory. The recorder must apply a delicate touch and develop a fine style of printing in recording information.

Like the Health block, the Family Background inventory is concerned with the *social* aspects of the response. For example, if a respondent had a sibling who died before the respondent's birth, the event obviously did not affect the respondent directly; consequently, information about the deceased sibling is *not* recorded. Only the sibling(s) with whom the respondent was reared or whom he or she knew are counted in this interview. (Siblings or children who were adopted are recorded as adopted to distinguish them from blood relatives.)

Figure 8-1 shows the position of the block on the recording sheet. Figure 8-2 shows the location of responses to the following items:

1. Reared in urban or rural setting
2. Parents alive or dead
3. Parents divorced or separated
4. Father's birthplace
5. Mother's birthplace
6. Father's occupation
7. Mother's occupation
8. Father's education
9. Mother's education
10. Father's age
11. Mother's age
12. Parents' relationship in respondent's teenage years
13. How get along with father
14. How get along with mother
15. Number of brothers and ages

16. Number of sisters and ages
17. Parochial grade school
18. Male friends at age 10–11
19. Female friends at age 10–11

Figure 8–3 (p. 60) shows the coded version of a typical family inventory.

Question 1

Have you ever lived on a farm continuously for at least a year?

Yes.

How old were you?

From about 11 to 18 years old.

FIGURE 8-2

1		
2	3	
4	5	
6	7	
8	9	
10	11	
12		
13	14	
15		
16	17	
18	19	

We define a farm as a place where crops or animals are grown for profit. The definition does not include an estate, a "place in the country," or a commune that is organized around crafts rather than agriculture or animal husbandry.

Although there are many reasons for asking whether the respondent's primary environmental background is urban or rural, three seem especially important. Initially, the information helps to identify who the respondent is and, to some degree, what her or his life has been like. Secondly, the information provides an additional peg in the framework system for identifying by association. Thirdly, the Kinsey research indicates that there are some differences in the effects of urban and rural living on a respondent's sex history: for example, the percentage of animal intercourse among males is much higher in rural communities. (This difference does not hold, however, for females.)

If the response is "no," the coding indicates that the respondent has lived in a city up to the time of the interview, i.e., city to date: **C-d**.

If the response is "yes," then the interview needs to get the respondent's age at the time. The information is recorded as **R** for rural plus respondent's age(s).

Question 2

Are your parents both living?

In recording the response, a check, ✓, means that both are alive. If either parent is dead, record which parent and the respondent's age at the time of parental death. In Figure 8–3, **M8** indicates that the mother died when the subject was age 8. If both parents are dead, record the respondent's age at the time of each parent's death as follows:

F4M5

Question 3

Are your parents living together?

or

Did your parents live together until your mother's (father's) death?

The third question is concerned with parental divorce or separation prior to the death of one of the parents. There is no need to indicate a difference between separation and divorce in recording information in this inventory because for our purposes it doesn't make that much difference—divorce is a legal term and has a similar effect on the respondent as would parental separation.

	Response Examples	*Recordings*
(a)	Yes.	**X**
	(i.e., no, they are not separated or divorced.)	

(b) No, they got divorced after I left   ↙
     home.
     (divorce during respondent's adult
     years.)

(c) No, they got divorced when I was nine   **9 lM X re**
     and I lived with my mother, who never
     remarried.
     (divorce during respondent's early
     years.)

(d) My biological father left when I was   **2 lM re 10-d**
     two, and I still live with my Mom, who
     remarried when I was 10.

(e) No, they split when I was 14. I lived   **14 lF re 15-18**
     with my Dad, who remarried when I
     was 15, until I left home after high
     school.

Note that an **X** here means just the reverse of what one might assume it to mean; that is, an **X** means "No, they are not separated or divorced," or "Yes, they are living together." This is one of the few places in the inventory where an **X** means yes.

If, indeed, the parents were not living together at the time of one of the parents' deaths, the respondent's age at the time of parental separation is checked and recorded as, for example, ↙**16**, meaning that the parents were separated or divorced when the respondent was aged 16.

The respondent frequently provides the answer to both Questions 2 and 3 when asked Question 2, as in the following examples:

Are both your parents living?

| *Response Examples* | *Recordings* |

(a) My parents are both living, in fact   ↙
     they're still living together.

(b) My father died when I was 23; my   **F 23 M 40 ↙ 20**
     mother died when I was 40. They sepa-
     rated when I was 20, and neither
     remarried.

(c) My father died when I was 5; I lived   **F 5 lM re-7**
     with my mother, who remarried when
     I was 7, and she's still living with my
     stepfather.

(d) I never knew my father. . . . I don't   **F? O! orph-12**
     know him now. . . . My parents were   **lM re-15**
     never married. I was sent to an or-   **lM-21**
     phanage until I was 12 years old. I
     went home to live with my Mom, who
     remarried when I was 15. She then

divorced and I continued to live with
her until I was 21.

(e) Oh, yes. Both my parents plus my   ∨ stpF lM re-3
stepfather are living. My parents
divorced when I was three, and my
mother married just after. But all
three have really raised me.
(The two fathers are recorded as of
equal influence.)

Questions 4 and 5

4. *Where was your father born?*

5. *Where was your mother born?*

If either the father or the mother was born outside the United States, record the
country of birth *plus* the parent's age at entering the United States; for example
Germ[US5] means the parent was born in Germany but came to the United States at the
age of 5.

Questions 6 and 7

6. *What was your father's occupation while you were living at home?*

7. *What was your mother's occupation while you were living at home?*

Because the questions are concerned with the social prestige of the occupations,
it's helpful to get job descriptions of such occupations as "engineer" and "salesperson," etc. An engineer can be anything from a janitor to a Ph.D., and a salesperson
can range from a pitchman to one responsible for a million dollars worth of sales
annually. Descriptions help identify the occupations' social prestige. These are recorded in the block in abbreviated writing.

Questions 8 and 9

8. *How far did your father go in school?*

9. *How far did your mother go in school?*

Questions 10 and 11

10. *How old is your father now?*

11. *What is your mother's age now?*

If the father or mother is dead, the interviewer determines how old the parent would be if he or she were living, records that age and circles it—e.g., ⑦⑧ —and then records the respondent's age at the time of the parent's death—e.g., ⑦⑧ **13.** In other words, the question asked is really, "How old would your father (or mother) be today if living?"

Question 12

How well did your parents get along with each other when you were a child at home?

Question 12 is concerned with the relationship between the parents when the respondent was living at home, particularly during his or her teenage years. If there were two parental marriages that were significant to the subject, record both.

Questions 13 and 14

13. *How did you get along with your father?*

14. *How did you get along with your mother?*

Questions 13 and 14 are concerned with the respondent's relationship with parents. Although the questions are rather perfunctory in this inventory, most interviewers will want to develop a whole series of questions about client relationships with other family members. The check system may be used in recording responses for these questions, unless the interviewer requires more detailed information.

Questions 15 and 16

15. *How many brothers do you have?*

    What are their ages?

16. *How many sisters do you have?*

    What are their ages?

These questions concern the siblings with whom the respondent *was raised* and their current ages. Again, the questions are concerned with the social definition of brothers and sisters, i.e., those male/female siblings who had a social impact on the respondent. If the respondent had a much older or younger sibling with whom there was little or no contact, that sibling would not be counted in this inventory.

A step- or half-sibling who was raised with the respondent or had some socialization impact on the respondent would be included, but recorded as (½) following the sibling's age, e.g., **2 = 17.15(½)**, meaning, two siblings, one age 17 and a half- or step-sibling age 15.

Adopted and foster children reared with the respondent are indicated by recording **AD** following the adopted sibling's age, e.g., **2 = 5.10AD**, meaning two siblings, one natural age 5 and the other age 10 and adopted.

If a sibling whom the respondent knew and was raised with has died, record the dead sibling's age if he or she were alive now, circled, and the age of the respondent at time of the sibling's death, e.g., ⑯ **12**, meaning that the sibling would be 16 if still alive and the respondent was 12 years old when he or she died. The recording of a response of three siblings, one adopted, one actual sibling age 14, and one who died when the respondent was 8 but who would be 21 if still alive would read: **3 = 16AD.14.** ㉑ **8.**

Question 17

Did you attend public grade school?

This question is concerned with whether or not the respondent attended a parochial *grade* school, that is, a school run by Catholics, Jews, Lutherans, Quakers, etc., and how old the respondent was while attending such a school.

Ask the follow-up question only if the response to the first part is "no."

The information might be recorded in the following way:

"No"	**X**
Catholic	**C** + ages
Lutheran	**Lth** + ages
Quaker	**Qkr** + ages
Jewish	**J** + ages

Questions 18 and 19

18. *When you were a child in fifth or sixth grade, did you have many playmates?*

19. *About how many were male?*

      and

About how many were female?

Questions 18 and 19 are concerned with the respondent's male and female friends at approximately 10 to 11 years of age.

Figure 8–3 (p. 60) shows how the following responses are coded. The subject is male, age 39, and never married.

1. *Have you ever lived on a farm continuously for a year?*

Well, I used to live with my grandparents on their old place. One time I lived on my uncle's ranch too.

How young were you when you lived with your grandparents?

I stayed with them about six months.

And how young were you when you lived with your uncle on his ranch?

It was when I got old enough to do heavy chores. I guess I was about 11.

How long did you live with your uncle then?

Until I graduated high school.

How old were you when you graduated.

18.

Fine.

2. *Are your parents both living?*

(3 answered here)

No, as I said, I went to live with my grandparents after my Ma died.

And as I recall, that was when you were 8?

Yep. My Dad's still alive, though.

Did you live with him until you moved to your uncle's ranch?

Yes. He'd come work the mowing season with us each year.

How long was the season?

Oh, just a few weeks.

4. *Where was your father born?*

Topeka.

5. *And where was your mother born?*

Well, she was born in Wilmington, Delaware.

6. *What was our father's occupation while you were living at home?*

Well, he worked sometimes with his brothers on the ranch helping out with the chores, but he's had a lot of different kinds of jobs.

7. *What did your mother do while you were living with her, before she died?*

She worked in a bakery.

8. *What is your father's education?*

He got through the sixth grade, I think.

9. *What is your mother's education?*

Oh, I'm pretty sure she finished high school but I don't really remember.

10. *How old is your father now?*

My dad must be about 68 today.

11. *And how old would your mother be today if she was living?*

Oh, I have no idea. She died when I was 8.

Do you know how long she and your father were together before you were born?

Well, I'm their first kid so I guess they knew each other a little while before they had me.

Do you know how old your mother was when she met your dad or when she got married to him?

Yes, she got married right out of high school, I remember them talking about that.

Then that means she was probably 25 when she died and you were 8. That is, if she graduated from high school around 17. Since you're 39, we can assume that she would have been 56. Does that sound about right?

Yeah, I guess that's about right, because she was younger than my dad.

12. *How well did your parents get along with each other when you were living at home?*

Well, they seemed to do okay. My mother was always bossing my dad around.

13. *How did you get along with your father?*

Well, my dad was sort of quiet so he was easy to get along with.

14. *How did you get along with your mother?*

We didn't get along so good. She was always punishing me for things I'd do.

15. *How many brothers do you have?*

I have two brothers, both younger than me.

What are their ages?

Stevie is 33 and Mike is 31.

16. *Do you have any sisters?*

I have one and she's just a year younger than me.

Oh, so she's 38?

Yeah.

17. *Did you attend public grade school?*

The nuns taught me when I first started school.

How long did the nuns teach you?

Until I went to live with my uncle.

And that was when you were 11, right?

That's right.

18, 19. *When you were a child in the fifth or sixth grade, did you have many playmates?*

Sure, I was really nuts about girls. But I had a lot of boyfriends too.

FIGURE 8-3

R 11-18		
M8	U 11-18	
Tpka	Wilm	
labr	bake	
6	12?	
68	⑤⑥8	
±		
✓	—	
2 = 31·33		
1 = 38 c√-11		
✓	✓	

BACKGROUND INFORMATION						
HEALTH			DREAMS		INCIDENTAL PROSTITUTION	
				PREMARITAL COITAL ATTITUDES		CONTRACEPTION
	EROTIC AROUSAL	PRE-ADOLESCENT SEX PLAY			EXTRA-MARITAL COITUS	
MARRIAGE			PREMARITAL PETTING	FIRST COITUS		INCIDENTAL HOMOSEXUALITY
		PUBERTY				
	FAMILY BACKGROUND				MARITAL COITUS	ANIMAL CONTACTS
ANATOMY		SELF-MASTURBATION	RECREATION	PREMARITAL COITUS		OTHER SEXUAL BEHAVIORS
	SEX EDUCATION		GROUP SEX			

FIGURE 9-1

9
Marriage

In our society, our marital status defines us to a significant degree. One is never married, married, separated, widowed, or divorced. Because marriage is so intertwined with sexual life, it is important to differentiate marital status in relation to sexual life.

Marriage is defined in the interview from a social point of view, not from a legal one. If a couple are legally married and living together, there is no question as to their marital status. If, however, they are legally married but not living together, they are considered separated. A couple who live together openly as husband and wife but are not legally married are considered married if they have lived together for a year or more and everyone knows about their arrangement. There may be combinations and variations of these arrangements. For example, a response of: "Well, I lived with him for two years and then we got married. We've been married for five years now," would be recorded as a seven year marriage.

If a subject has been married more than once, the Marriage block is divided vertically (Figure 9-2) and each question is asked separately with regard to each marriage. If there are more than three marriages, a supplementary form should be used. In special situations, such as group marriage, the interviewer will have to determine his or her own definition of each respondent's status.

Figure 9-1 shows the location of the block in relation to other blocks and Figure 9-2 shows the location of the coded responses to the following thirteen questions in this block:

1. Age at marriage
2. Age of spouse at marriage
3. Length of marriage
4. Is respondent living with spouse
5. Number and ages of sons

6. Number and ages of daughters
7. How long after marriage was the first child born
8. Other pregnancies in the marriage
9. How long did respondent know spouse before marriage
10. Length of announced engagement
11. Education of spouse
12. Religion of spouse during marriage and degree of devotion
13. Respondent's rating of marital happiness

Figure 9–3 shows the coding of the responses given in the following interview:

Question 1

How old were you when you were married?

I was 22.

Question 2

All right, how old was your husband?

27.

Question 3

How long have you been married?

We've been married fourteen years.

Question 4

Are you presently living with your spouse?

Yes.

This question is really concerned with whether the respondent is not separated, divorced or widowed. Therefore an **X** in this case means that the respondent is still living with her spouse and a check means that she is not. The question is concerned with when they stopped living together, not when they were divorced, even though the divorce may have taken a year or more before it became final.

FIGURE 9-2

1		
2		
3		
4		
5		
6		
7		
8		
9		
10		
11		
12		
13		

FIGURE 9-3

22		
27		
14y		
X		
2= 3·9		
3= 2·5·14		
5 M		
ab@32+sp@32		
1y		
4 M		
14 → 20		
C —		
1 → 3		

Question 5

How many sons do you have?`

Two.

What are their ages?

3 and 9.

Question 6

How many daughters do you have?
Three.

What are their ages?
2, 5 and 14.

Question 7

How long were you married before your first child was born?
She came along five months after we were married.

This question may pick up "forced" marriages.

Question 8

How many other pregnancies were there in the marriage?
I had one abortion last year and a miscarriage four years ago.

All right.

Sp means a spontaneous abortion or miscarriage, **ab** means an induced abortion.

Question 9

How long did you know your spouse existed before you were married?
We met at work. I knew him about a year.

Question 10

Was there an announced engagement?
Yes.

How long were you engaged?
4 months.

Question 11

What is your spouse's education?
He was a sophomore in college when we were married and now he is a medical doctor.

If the educational status has changed during the marriage, the amount of education at the beginning of the marriage and the amount of education presently or at the end of the marriage are both recorded.

Question 12

What is your spouse's religion?

He is Catholic.

How often does he attend church?

Once a year. Christmas Mass.

Question 13

On a scale from 1 to 4, with 1 being very happy and 4 being very unhappy, how would you rate your marriage? This includes how it started out and where it is now.

When we were first married, it was a 1 but now I guess it is a 3. Things aren't as good as they used to be.

HEALTH			DREAMS	INCIDENTAL PROSTITUTION	
		PRE- ADOLESCENT SEX PLAY		PREMARITAL COITAL ATTITUDES	CONTRACEPTION
	EROTIC AROUSAL			EXTRA- MARITAL COITUS	
MARRIAGE			PREMARITAL PETTING	FIRST COITUS	INCIDENTAL HOMOSEXUALITY
		PUBERTY			
	FAMILY BACKGROUND			MARITAL COITUS	ANIMAL CONTACTS
ANATOMY		SELF- MASTURBATION	RECREATION	PREMARITAL COITUS	OTHER SEXUAL BEHAVIORS
	SEX EDUCATION		GROUP SEX		

FIGURE 10-1

10
Sex Education

The Sex Education block is the first part of the history that begins to tap specific information about sex. Because the focus is on how the respondent learned about various aspects of sex rather than on his or her overt behavior, the block provides a relatively unintimidating introduction to the inquiry into sexual behavior. Asking about one's sex education is usually nonthreatening because no one is responsible for his or her sex education.

One of the purposes of the Sex Education block is to introduce sexual vocabulary for the first time in the interviewing inventory—words such as intercourse, venereal disease, homosexuality, etc. Often, this is the first time the respondent has heard or said many words associated with sex. Such verbalization reveals a wealth of information on how the subject acquired early "facts" about sex and sexuality. The interviewer can often pick up attitudes toward sex that are clues to the subject's behavior in adult life. For example, hesitation, embarrassment, or lack of eye contact may suggest that the subject may be resistive or even noncooperative when it comes to discussing his or her overt behavior. If the subject, conversely, responds in an aggressive or seductive manner to such words as intercourse, penis, etc., the interviewer may expect a more elaborate sexual history than usual. At any rate, one can often pick up clues to a subject's overt sexual history by the reaction the subject displays in talking about early sex education.

In the process of obtaining sex education information, the interviewer is not only delving for information but also using the opportunity, if appropriate, to educate the subject. The introduction of sexual terminology often provides the interviewer the opportunity to define and explain terms—an educational process in itself—and gives the respondent an opportunity to acquire new information or to clarify existing information.

In exploring the subject's sex education, the interviewer asks the age at which the subject recalls learning about the behavior. The question is phrased, "How young were you when . . . ," as opposed to "how old" because people tend to remember such events as acquiring sexual information as occurring at older ages than was in fact the case.

There are a number of major sources from which almost everyone acquired early sex knowledge. These sources and the appropriate coding are as follows:

Sources	Code
peers	**P**
adults	**Pa**
books	**B**
teacher	**T**
mother	**M**
father	**F**
brother	**Br**
sister	**Sis**
animals	**Z**
movies	**Mov**
self-discovery	**Slf**
event	**Ev**

The Sex Education block is a good area in which to establish sexual awareness pegs. For example, when asked, "How young were you when you first learned that the baby grows inside the mother?" the respondent might say, "I can't remember." An appropriate follow-up question might be, "Can you remember what grade you were in?" or "Were you still living in Topeka?" or "Did you know it before your brother was born?" The answers to these questions can enable the interviewer to calculate an approximate age, which he or she immediately checks with the respondent. This question and answer exchange in the process of building pegs helps establish a frame of reference for further recall by the respondent.

Figure 10-1 shows the location of the Sex Education block in relation to the others. There are sixteen items in this block, recorded in the locations indicated in Figure 10-2. The items concern the following topics, listed, as usual, in the sequence in which the questions are asked:

1. Pregnancy and source of information
2. Intercourse and source of information
3. Menstruation and source of information
4. Sexually transmitted disease and source of information
5. Gonorrhea
6. Syphilis
7. (a) Herpes
   (b) Monilia
   (c) Trichomonas vaginalis
8. Condoms and source of information

9. Prostitution and source of information
10. Homosexuality and source of information
11. Father as information source
12. Mother as information source
13. Teacher as information source
14. Major source of information
15. Nudity as a child
16. Nude sleeping now

FIGURE 10-2

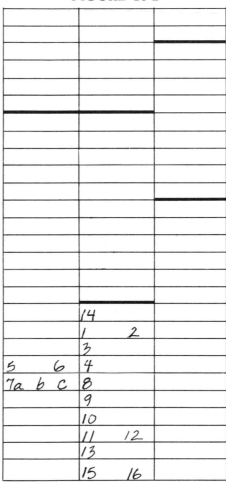

Question 1

How young were you when you first learned that the baby grows inside the mother?

The question is simply worded so that it can be used at all educational levels. The phrasing "baby grows inside the mother" is used to prevent confusion of pregnancy with conception; "baby grows inside the mother" conveys a concise image to everyone.

The response is very often a frustrated "I have no idea," or "I just can't remember." Instead of accepting such a response, the interviewer should push the respondent to make a wild guess. Such guesses have been shown to be reliable even though their validity may not be provable. That is, they will probably remain the same during follow-up interviews. The Kinsey research found that upon retaking sex histories after several years, the respondents, still protesting that they were guessing, continued to guess very close to the original response.*

The interviewer records not only the age of the respondent at the time the knowledge was acquired but also the source of the information.

How did you learn about it?

Question 2

How young were you when you first learned that the penis can go inside the vagina?

When interviewing a sophisticated, upper social level person, the interviewer would use the word "intercourse" because it seems obvious that the respondent would know the meaning. At very low social levels, the question might be,

When did you first know there was fucking?

Some lower social level blacks use "intercourse" as a verb ("I intercoursed her," or "We intercoursed"). Hence, the appropriate question might be,

When did you first learn about intercoursing? How did you learn about it?

Question 3

How young were you when you first knew there was such a thing as menstruation?

The use of euphemisms such as "falling off the roof," "having my friend," "getting my period," "having the rag on," "riding a white horse" is counterproductive for both respondent and interviewer. While interviewing a subject of a lower social level, however, the interviewer may want to adopt the subject's mispronunciation of the word menstruation as "ministration." It is better to go along with the mispronunciation because correction may interfere with rapport and inhibit responses.

If the respondent is a female, the interviewer may want to go from the menstruation question directly to the Puberty block and ask, "How young were you when you first menstruated?" With a male history, this jump, of course, doesn't apply. An example of the question sequence, response, and appropriate coding of this jump from information in one block to information in another follows:

When did you first know that women bleed regularly through the vagina?
I didn't know about it until I started at 11.

I see.

*A.C. Kinsey, W.B. Pomeroy, and C.E. Martin, *Sexual Behavior in the Human Male* (Philadelphia: W.B. Saunders, 1948), p. 123.

This response would be recorded as **11 Ev**, meaning 11 years of age owing to an event, and at the same time recorded in the Puberty block as **11** on the second line, for age of menarche.

For this question and for the others in this block, the respondent is also asked to identify the source of his or her information, unless the source is volunteered as part of the response to the earlier question.

Question 4

How young were you when you first learned there was such a thing as gonorrhea or syphilis?

For lower social levels, the question might be,

When did you first know there was such a thing as a dose of clap or bad blood?

Question 4 is concerned with knowledge about sexually transmitted diseases. The questions asked use the names of gonorrhea and syphilis because most people know these terms rather than the categorical name, venereal disease.

At this point, depending on the respondent's manner, the interviewer has to make a subjective judgment: is this the appropriate moment in the history to ask whether the respondent has ever had gonorrhea or syphilis? When interviewing a person who appears unresponsive and not really at ease, it might be prudent to skip the question at this point of the interview. One must remember, of course, to return to it at a later time when the respondent may feel more comfortable. If a person seems to be relaxed, friendly, open, and "with it" in terms of responding to the interview, a second judgment to be made is whether to phrase the question, "Have you ever had gonorrhea?" or "Have you ever had syphilis?" or to make the assumption by phrasing it, "How young were you when you first had gonorrhea [or syphilis]?"

These judgments that the interviewer must make are based on extremely subtle, often subliminal clues. If the interviewer is not sure, it is better to postpone the question. It must be asked eventually, but there are some built-in reminders to prompt the interviewer to get this information. One is that the information is located in the Anatomy block, and in the process of asking the anatomy questions, the interviewer will be reminded to ask about VD. Another built-in reminder comes from the Premarital Coitus block. One possible answer from the checklist of responses to the question "Why didn't you have more premarital intercourse?" is "fear of venereal disease." Here again, the interviewer has a convenient opportunity to ask the respondent about sexually transmitted diseases.

Questions 5, 6, and 7

5. *Have you ever had gonorrhea?*

    or

Have you ever had a dose of clap?

If the answer is positive then these additional questions are asked:

6. *When did you have gonorrhea?*

    or

When did you get your first dose?

    and

Did you get it from a male or a female?

Question 7 is concerned with whether or not the respondent has had other sexually transmitted diseases, specifically herpes, monilia, and trichomonas vaginitis. Question phrasing is the same as in asking about gonorrhea and syphilis.

Question 8

How young were you when you first knew there was such a thing as a rubber safety, or a rubber condom?

The terms "rubber safety" or "rubber condom" are less ambiguous than the euphemism "rubber," which can be misinterpreted or misunderstood.

Question 9

How young were you when you first knew that there was such a thing as prostitution or that women were paid money for intercourse?

Note that this question is concerned with knowledge of prostitution, not experience.

Question 10

How young were you the first time you knew there was such a thing as homosexuality?

    or

How young were you when you found out that two males or two females could have sex with each other?

Questions 11 and 12

Of interest here is the parent's contribution to the respondent's sex education:

11. *How much did your father contribute to your sex education?*

12. *How much did your mother contribute to your sex education?*

Asking "how much" prevents the respondent from giving an unqualified yes or no answer, as would be the typical reply to "Did your father (or mother) contribute to your sex education?" The check system is used to indicate quantity.

Question 13

How much did teachers in school contribute to your sex education?

Use the check system to indicate quantity.

Question 14

From what source would you say you got most of your sex education?

or

What was your major source of sex education?

or

Where did you get most of your sex information?

Question 15

As a small child—say, older than three—were you allowed to run around the house without any clothes on?

Lower social level phrasing might be:

Were you allowed to run around buck naked?

If the respondent asks, "How young?" an answer to the question is anything the respondent can remember past the age of three. (A child of less than three would not qualify for nudity in terms of this question.)

Question 16

Do you sleep in the nude now?

Lower social level phrasing might be:

Do you sleep naked now?

Use check system to record quantity.

Examples of Responses and Coding

A. *Female, college-educated, age 48 (see Figure 10–3)*

1. *How young were you the first time you learned the baby grows inside the mother?*

   Well, I suppose that was when my brother was born and I was 5 years old.

   Did your mother tell you about it?

   No, I just saw her getting bigger and I just figured it out for myself.

   I understand.

2. *When did you first learn that there was such a thing as intercourse?*

   Well, I read about it when I was 12.

FIGURE 10-3. Female

Yes, but before that, did you know?

Yes, I had some idea that the penis goes in the vagina, I guess around 7. A friend of mine told me.

O.K.

3. *When did you first know that women bleed regularly from the vagina?*

Oh, I didn't have any idea about that until I was 12, and my older sister told me about it.

All right.

4. *When did you first know that there was such a thing as gonorrhea or syphilis?*

Well, I read about that in a book. Oh no, I saw a movie about it when I was 13.

5. *Have you ever had gonorrhea?*

Once, when I was 17. I got it from my boyfriend.

6. *Have you ever had syphilis?*

No, never.

7. *(a) Have you ever had herpes?*

Oh, I had that twice, one on my upper lip, and one other time on my genitals.

How young were you when you had it on your genitals?

I was about 15.

How did you contract it?

It just came by itself.

(b) Have you ever had monilia?

I'm not sure. I itch and burn down there sometimes after a lot of intercourse.

What do you do about it when you have the itching and burning?

Oh, nothing but take a bath and not have intercourse for a few days until it goes away.

(c) Have you ever had trichomonas vaginitis?

I don't even know what it is.

O.K.

8. *Okay, when did you first know that there were rubber condoms?*

I saw one lying in the street when I was 8 years old.

Did you know what it was for?

No, I thought it was a balloon.

Well, when did you first really know what condoms were?

I was 12 when my friends told me about that.

9. *How young were you when you first knew that women were paid for intercourse?*

Oh, the other kids told me when I was about 14.

10. *When did you know there was such a thing as homosexuality?*

Oh, I realized that the first time I had it.

There is no need to record this information in the Homosexuality block because it will routinely be asked again. The interviewer does, however, make a mental note of the fact.

How old were you?

I was 11.

All right

11. *Did your father give you much sex information?*

No. He tried to once, but he just wasn't able to say much.

12. *Did your mother give you any sex information?*

Very little.

13. *How much did teachers in high school or grade school contribute to your sex education?*

I had a little bit in class in high school, just a little.

14. *What was your major source of sex education?*

Well, I suppose that friends gave me most of my information, but my father told me not to get pregnant.

15. *As a small child, were you allowed to run around the house with no clothing?*

Oh, I think a little, I remember just vaguely.

16. *Do you sleep in the nude now?*

No, but I used to when I was younger.

B. *Male, eighth-grade education, age 30 (see Figure 10–4)*

1. *How young were you when you first learned that the baby grows inside the mother?*

Gee, I've always known that.

Well, make a guess. About how young do you think you were?

Oh, maybe 7 years old.

And how did you learn about that?

Oh, the kids around the block.

FIGURE 10-4. Male

	14 P	
	1 7P Z7P	
	3 12A	
5 13♀ 6x	4 13EV	
7	8 12	
	9 12 P.	
	10 15P	
	11 X 12xtry	
	13X 16X	
	15x	

2. *And when did you first learn about fucking?*
I must have know that about the same time.

3. *When did you first learn that girls bleed every month?*
Oh, I didn't know that until I was real old.

About how old do you think?
Oh, maybe 12.

And how did you learn that?
From—my aunt told me that.

4. *All right, when did you first learn there was such a thing as clap or bad blood?*
I first had clap when I was 13.

5. *No, when did you first know about the clap?*
Oh, I knew about it when I got it.

6. *All right, you were 13, and did you get it from a male or female?*
I got it from a whore down the block.

And have you had bad blood or syphilis?
No, I've never had that.

8. *When did you first know about rubber safeties or rubber condoms?*
Oh, I saw those around the neighborhood when I was around 12 years old.

9. *And when did you first know that women get paid for fucking?*
Oh, I was about the same age, 12.

How did you learn that?
From the other guys.

10. *When did you first learn that boys could have sex with other boys?*
Oh, I ain't never done that.

No, but when did you first know that it was possible?
Oh, I heard the guys talking about queers—I was about 12.

11. *Did you get any sex information from your father?*
No, he never told me nothing.

12. *And how about from your mother?*

    Oh, she tried to tell me a little bit but I already knew more than she did.

13. *And how about from your schoolteacher?*

    No, never heard nothing from them.

14. *How did you learn most about sex?*

    Oh, from the other guys in the neighborhood.

15. *As a small child, were you allowed to run around the house without any clothes on?*

    Jesus, no.

16. *And do you sleep naked now?*

    No, I always wear my shorts.

BACKGROUND INFORMATION

HEALTH			DREAMS		INCIDENTAL PROSTITUTION	
				PREMARITAL COITAL ATTITUDES		CONTRACEPTION
	EROTIC AROUSAL	PRE-ADOLESCENT SEX PLAY			EXTRA-MARITAL COITUS	
MARRIAGE						
			PREMARITAL PETTING	FIRST COITUS		INCIDENTAL HOMOSEXUALITY
		PUBERTY				
	FAMILY BACKGROUND				MARITAL COITUS	ANIMAL CONTACTS
ANATOMY		SELF-MASTURBATION	RECREATION	PREMARITAL COITUS		OTHER SEXUAL BEHAVIORS
	SEX EDUCATION		GROUP SEX			

FIGURE 11-1

11

Puberty

Puberty or pubescence is that time in a child's life when physically he or she develops secondary sex characteristics and when the reproductive organs become functional. Puberty is thought of as lasting only a few months but it is the beginning of adolescence, which may last for many years.

This is the time in the life cycle when people are concerned with their sexual awakenings and desires. It is an age when peer influence and comparison are of major concern and when one begins to define life values. In addition to the concern about physiological changes and the increased surge of hormones in the bloodstream, the pubescent individual is often obsessed with behavior problems and the sexual question, "Am I normal?" At this time, females are also concerned about first menses and growth of breasts, males about first ejaculation, growth of penis, growth of beard, and voice changes. Of concern to both sexes are pubic hair and the period of rapid growth.

There are fifteen questions in the Puberty block, but several are asked only of males or only of females, and the answer to one, Question 10, is estimated by the interviewer after all the other questions in the block have been answered.

The location of the block is shown in Figure 11–1. Figure 11–2 shows the location of the coded responses to the following questions:

1. Age at first ejaculation (male) or at onset of menarche (female)
2. How ejaculation occurred (male only)
3. Age at first orgasm
4. How orgasm occurred
5. Age first pubic hair appeared
6. Age at cessation of rapid growth

7. Age when voice change (male only)
8. Age at breast development (female only)
9. Feelings about breast development (female only)
10. Estimated age of puberty (interviewer)
11. Age at graduation from high school.
12. Type of high school
13. Number of male friends when 15 or 16 years old
14. Number of female friends when 15 or 16 years old
15. Age when moved out of the family home

FIGURE 11-2

		10	
		1 2	
		3 4	
		5 6	
		7	
		8 9	
		11 12	
		13 14	
		15	

Question 1

Males are asked:

How young were you the first time you ever ejaculated?

   or

How young were you the first time you came?

   or

How young were you the first time the white stuff came out of your cock?

Females are asked:

How young were you when you started menstruating?

   or

How young were you when you had your first period?

   Most women remember when they had their first menstrual period. When a respondent has had a long delay in menstruation and all of the signs of pubescence are there, like breast development and pubic hair, there may be an endocrine or an anorexic problem. Onset of menstruation depends on body weight, and a girl who is very thin may not begin to menstruate until later.

Question 2

How did the ejaculation occur?

   Masturbation is the answer given by 90 percent of the respondents. Ejaculation can also occur during nocturnal emission, coitus, petting, homosexual contact, animal contact, and spontaneously.
   Most males ejaculate within a year of puberty. If there is a male who goes for a long period of time after adolescence without ejaculation, look for a situation of psychological inhibition or an endocrine problem.

Question 3

How young were you when you had the feeling of orgasm or coming before you ever ejaculated?

   or

Before you ever ejaculated, did you ever have a feeling of coming?

   Some males experience preadolescent orgasm and this should be investigated.

Question 4

How did the orgasm occur?

   or

How did it happen?

   If the response to question 3 is "I never had the feeling of orgasm before my first ejaculation," then there is no need to ask question 4. It would be assumed that first orgasm and first ejaculation occurred at the same time.

Question 3 (asked of female)

How young were you the first time you experienced orgasm?

or

How young were you the first time you were able to come?

or

How young were you the first time you came to climax?

Question 4

How did the orgasm occur?

Question 5

How young were you when pubic hair first began to grow?

Many males are surprised by the question because they hadn't given much thought to their pubic hair. Women are sometimes asked:

How young were you when the hair began to grow down there?

This is one of the rare exceptions to the rule against using euphemisms. Kinsey found that lower social level women in particular were greatly offended by his use of the term "pubic hair" and therefore used this euphemism.

If given time to reflect, most women will remember having pubic hair before their breasts began to develop or at the same time. Most will remember that they had pubic hair at the onset of menstruation.

Question 6

How young were you when you stopped growing rapidly in height?

It is between puberty and 16 that males may grow five, six, or seven inches in one year. They may be awkward, gawky, and uncoordinated. Most females grow rapidly at 14, 15, and 16 years of age.

Question 7 (males only)

How young were you when your voice began to change?

During this period the high prepubescent voice will become lower in pitch and more resonant in tone. This may occur over a period of months or longer. Often the male has no control over the pitch of his voice. It may crack and squeak and be a cause of embarrassment to him. There are, however, males who have very little memory of this change. Very often the best peg is singing in a school choir, when the voice changes from a soprano to an alto, tenor, or bass.

Question 8 (females only)

How young were you when your breasts first began to grow?

Question 9

How did you feel about it?

	Speedwriting
Proud?	**Prd**
Indifferent?	**Indf**
Embarrassed?	**Emb**

Question 10

Note that the age of puberty is not asked of the respondent but is completed by the interviewer after all questions are answered. The interviewer's estimate of the age of puberty is a very important peg because there are many behaviors that relate to before or after puberty. This estimation is based on the respondent's recall of his or her age at the manifestation of pubic hair, first ejaculation, menses, breast development, and/or voice change. From this information the interviewer is able to make a fairly accurate judgment of age at puberty.

Question 11

How old were you when you graduated from high school?

Question 12

Was this a private or a public high school?

Question 13

About how many male friends did you have when you were 15 and 16?

CHECK SYSTEM

⌐	a lot of friends
±	some
—	few
X	none

Question 14

How many female friends did you have when you were 15 and 16?

Question 15

How old were you when you no longer thought of your parents' home as yours?

Examples of Responses and Coding

A. *Male, college-educated, age 37 (see Figure 11–3)*

1. *How young were you the first time you came?*

   It was just after my thirteenth birthday.

FIGURE 11-3.   Male

		13	
		13	M
		12	H
		11	16
		14	
		0	0
		18	HS
		±	—
		22	

Fine.

2. *How did it happen?*

I was lying in bed one night rubbing my penis and I suddenly came.

3. *Before you ever ejaculated, did you ever have a feeling of coming?*

I think it was about a year before my first ejaculation.

You were about 12 then?

Yes.

4. *How did the orgasm happen?*

I was fooling around with my friend John.

5. *How young were you when pubic hair first began to grow?*

I don't remember.

Make a guess.

Shortly before I came.

Your first orgasm was at 12.

Yes, I guess I noticed pubic hair the summer I was 11, because I remember seeing my cousin Joe had it too.

O.K.

6. *How young were you when you stopped growing rapidly in height?*

I was in tenth or eleventh grade, I think.

You were about 15 or 16?

I think closer to 16.

7. *How young were you when your voice began to change?*

I guess it happened when people mistook me for my dad on the phone.

How old were you then?

I was in high school—I guess about ninth grade.

You were about 14?

Yes, I think so.

Fine.

11. *How old were you when you graduated from high school?*

I was just 18. I remember celebrating by having my first legal beer.

12. *Was this a private or a public high school?*

A public school.

13. *About how many male friends did you have when you were 15 and 16?*

I had a friend.

Would you say you had a lot of friends, or were you a loner?

Well, I had one real buddy, and we palled around with three other guys.

So you would say you had about four friends?

Guess so.

14. *About how many female friends did you have when you were 15 and 16?*

I never really dated in high school.

Did you have any girls that you would talk with on a daily basis?

No, not really, but there was my cousin Joan. We were good friends.

So you are saying Joan was your only female friend in high school?

Yes, I liked her.

15. *How old were you when you no longer thought of your parents' home as yours?*

Well, I went away to college when I was 18, but I came home for vacations.

Did you feel that you still lived at home?

Yes, I really did. I didn't leave, I guess, until I went to graduate school. Then I moved out and didn't come to their home every vacation.

You graduated high school at 18? How old were you when you entered graduate school?

I was 22—four years later.

B. *Female, college-educated, age 23 (see Figure 11–4)*

1. *How young were you when you had your first period?*

I was 11 years old.

Fine.

FIGURE 11-4. Female

		13	
		13	O
		12	P
		12	15
		O	
		11	PRD
		17	PS
		✓	I
		18	

3. *How young were you the first time you experienced orgasm?*

   I was about 13. I remember it well.

4. *How did the orgasm occur?*

   My boyfriend was finger-fucking me and I was standing up—all of a sudden my whole body began to jump and I felt warm all over.

5. *How young were you when the hair began to grow down there?*

   About the time I began menstruating.

   You were about 11?

   Yes.

   Fine.

6. *How young were you when you stopped growing rapidly in height?*

   I was 15. Thank goodness I stopped!

8. *How young were you when your breasts first began to grow?*

   I was in the sixth grade when I noticed my nipples were beginning to look bigger than they had. One of my friends told me I should wear a bra.

   You were 11?

   Yes.

   O.K.

9. *How did you feel about it?*

   I was delighted. My sisters had told me that boys liked big breasts, and I wanted boys to like me.

   So you were pleased.

   Yes.

   O.K.

11. *How old were you when you graduated from high school?*

    I was 17.

12. *Was this a private or a public high school?*

    A private girls' school.

13. *About how many male friends did you have when you were 15 and 16?*

    About four.

14. *How many female friends did you have when you were 15 and 16?*

    I had three dear friends. We had our share of fights, but we are still friends today.

15. *How old were you when you no longer thought of your parents' home as yours?*

    18.

BACKGROUND INFORMATION

HEALTH			DREAMS		INCIDENTAL PROSTITUTION	
				PREMARITAL COITAL ATTITUDES		CONTRACEPTION
	EROTIC AROUSAL	PRE-ADOLESCENT SEX PLAY			EXTRA-MARITAL COITUS	
MARRIAGE						
			PREMARITAL PETTING	FIRST COITUS		INCIDENTAL HOMOSEXUALITY
		PUBERTY				
	FAMILY BACKGROUND				MARITAL COITUS	ANIMAL CONTACTS
ANATOMY				PREMARITAL COITUS		
		SELF-MASTURBATION	RECREATION			OTHER SEXUAL BEHAVIORS
	SEX EDUCATION					
			GROUP SEX			

FIGURE 12-1

12

Preadolescent Sex Play

There are people who have forgotten their preadolescent sex play because it was inconsequential and others who have repressed their experiences because they were traumatic. But many people have very vivid and clear memories of their early sexual experiences. A knowledge of early sexual experience helps to round out the individual's sexual history. In therapy, especially sex therapy, information about preadolescent sex play can be of tremendous help to the clinician in understanding some of the person's current problems for such experiences may be an indicator of early attitude development. An exploration of early sex experiences is therefore a necessary part of any sex history interview.

Most people respond very readily to questions about their preadolescent sex play because they do not feel responsible for behavior that occurred when they were too young to consider the behavior taboo. It is interesting that the Kinsey interviewers, when exploring early preadolescent sex play with very young children, discovered that it was easier for the children to reveal their early homosexual experiences than their early heterosexual experiences. The reason was that the children had not picked up taboos against homosexual behavior but had been cautioned against heterosexual behavior. As people develop an awareness of the taboos about homosexuality, they then shift their willingness to discuss their early preadolescent sex play to heterosexual behavior.

Extensive early homosexual sex play that continues through adolescence is frequently an indicator of homosexuality. There are many people, however, who experience early homosexual sex play which does not continue throughout adolescence and therefore is not indicative of homosexual orientation.

For the purposes of this inventory, preadolescent sex play is defined as genital sex play and does not include hugging, kissing, or fondling of breasts.

The location of the Preadolescent Sex Play block is indicated in Figures 12–1. The questions in this block are divided into four groups, as illustrated in Figure 12–2. The top half of the block is concerned with sex play with females, the bottom half with males. A vertical line distinguishes preadolescent sex play with peers from preadolescent sex play with adults. In other words, Questions 1 through 7 concern preadolescent sex play with young females and are recorded in the upper left-hand quarter of the block; Questions 15 through 21 are concerned with preadolescent sex play with adult females and are recorded in the upper right-hand quarter of the block. Similarly, Questions 8 through 14 are concerned with preadolescent sex play with young males and are recorded in the lower left quarter of the block; Questions 22 through 28 concern preadolescent sex play with adult males and are recorded in

FIGURE 12-2

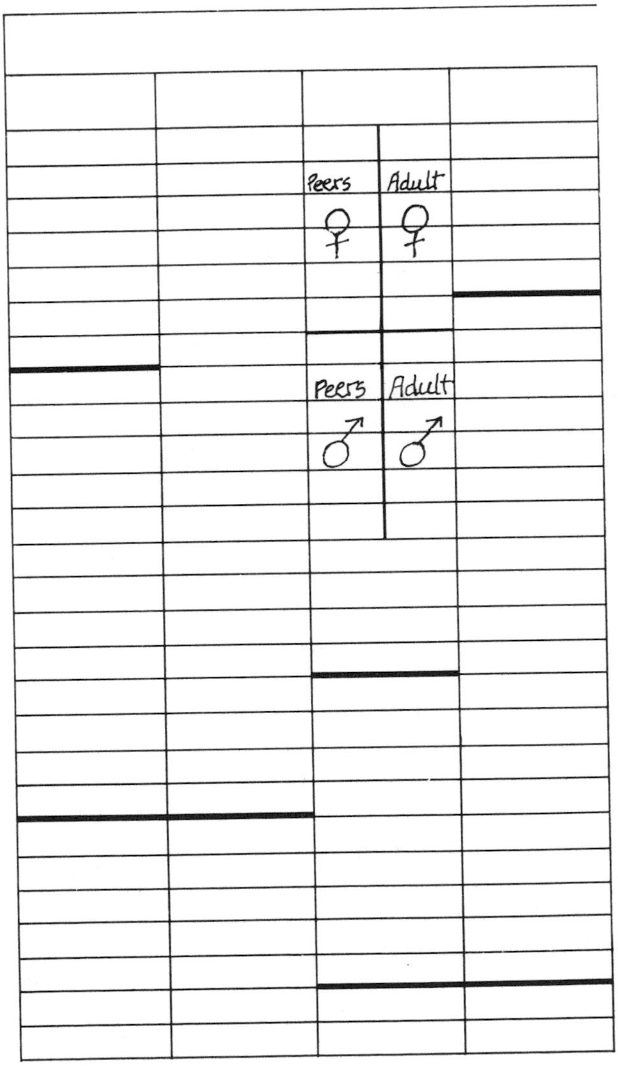

the lower right-hand quarter of the block. Responses to Questions 29 and 30 are recorded at the bottom of the block (see Figure 12–3).

When taking the sex history of a male respondent, the top half of this block will reflect the respondent's heterosexual experiences and the bottom part of the block his homosexual experiences. Conversely, when taking the sex history of a female respondent, the top half will reflect homosexual activities and the bottom part heterosexual experiences.

Although there are relatively few incidents of preadolescent sex play with adult females, early sex play with adult males is common for both male and female respondents. In addition to identifying the behaviors, the interviewer will be interested in the respondent's age at the time of the sex play, the frequency of experiences, his or her descriptions and reactions at the time of the experience, and whether or not the respondent has ever told anybody else about the experience.

FIGURE 12-3

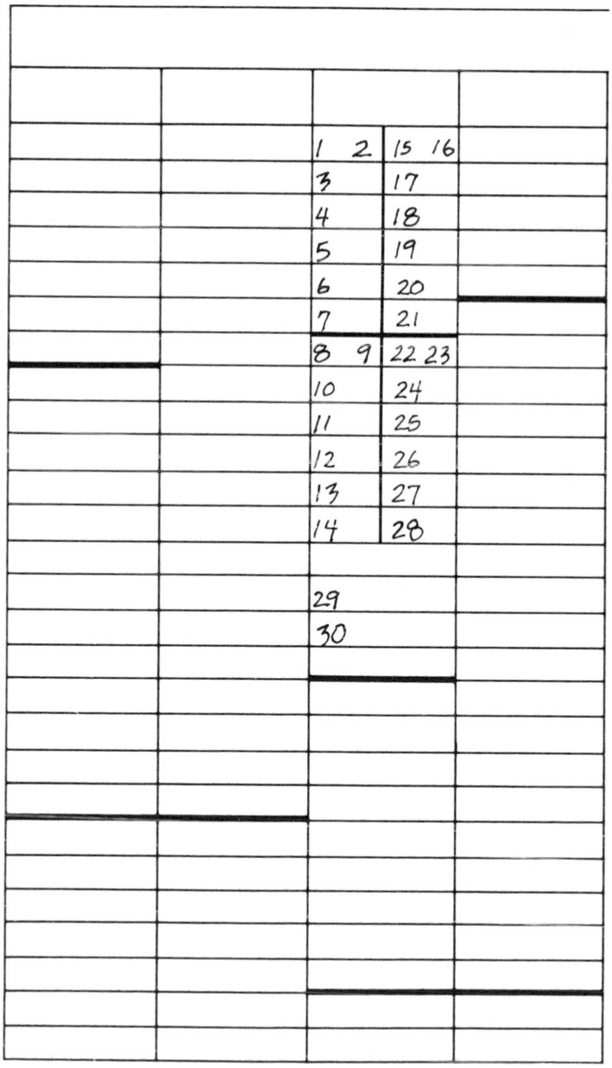

The questions asked in this block are as follows:

1. Age of first peer ♀ sex play	17. Show
2. Frequency	18. Touch
3. Show	19. Objects in vagina
4. Touch	20. Oral-genital stimulation
5. Objects in vagina	21. Coital attempts
6. Oral-genital stimulation	22. Age of first adult ♂ sex play
7. Coital attempts	23. Frequency
8. Age of first peer ♂ sex play	24. Show
9. Frequency	25. Touch
10. Show	26. Oral-genital stimulation
11. Touch	27. Urethral stimulation
12. Oral-genital stimulation	28. Anal insertion
13. Urethral insertion	29. Age when first saw preadolescent genitalia of opposite sex
14. Anal insertion	
15. Age of first adult ♀ sex play	30. Age when first saw adult genitalia of opposite sex
16. Frequency	

Question 1

How young were you the first time there was ever any sex play with another female?

Question 2

How frequently did you have genital sex play?

It is important for the interviewer to identify the total number of partners involved during the preadolescent sex play exercises. The additional information concerning a summary of partners involved might be asked in the following way,

How many children did you have genital play with?

Questions 3 through 7 are concerned with techniques of sex play—showing genitals, touching genitals, inserting objects into the vagina, oral-genital experiences, and intercourse (including attempts).

In taking the sex history, the interviewer should distinguish between activities experienced by the respondent in a passive way and those in which he or she engaged in an active way. The interviewer may record on the appropriate line **a** for active, **p** for passive, or **m** for mutual (that is, both active and passive). In interpreting these notations, **a** means that the respondent showed his or her genitalia, **p** means that the respondent was shown someone else's genitalia, and **m** means that both partners showed their genitalia.

The phrasing of Questions 4 through 7 may follow the same illustrations listed here for Question 3:

3. *Was there any showing of sex organs?*

or

Did you show your sex organs?

and

Did you see other children's genitals?

Questions 8 through 14 continue in the same format as the previous questions but refer to preadolescent sex play with young males. Questions 8 through 11 are identical in content to Questions 1 through 4 except for the partner's gender. Questions 12, 13, and 14, however, are concerned with oral-genital experience, urethral insertion, and anal insertion. They are asked in the same manner as are the techniques for sex play with young females.

Questions 15 through 28 elicit the identical information as Questions 1 through 14 but are concerned with sex play between the respondent as a preadolescent and an adult. An adult is defined in this inventory as postpubescent and five or more years older than the respondent. Thus, a 15-year-old having sex play with a 12-year-old (prepubescent) would not qualify as an adult by this definition, but if the partner of the 15-year-old was 8 years of age, then the older person would qualify as an adult.

As adult sex play with preadolescents is not nearly so frequent as peer sex play, the interviewer may find it unnecessary to ask all the questions on this side of the block. The interviewer may find it more expedient simply to take down the respondent's description of sex play with adult contacts in speedwriting or some form of shorthand. For instance, the respondent may report an experience with a man, thought to be about 45 years of age, who grabbed the respondent once when he was 12 years old, and touched his penis; the respondent got very frightened and was afraid to tell anyone about it. Such a response might look something like the following:

1 X ♂ = 45 grbGs = frite X tell

A female respondent at age 11 sees a man exhibiting himself on the subway and is amused. This example might be recorded as follows:

11 sub ♂ exh amuse

Questions 29 and 30 ask how old (young) the respondent was the first time he or she saw the genitals of a preadolescent and of an adult member of the opposite sex. For Question 30, an adult is defined as anyone with pubic hair. The questions are generally asked in the following way:

29. *How young were you the first time you ever saw a young girl's (or boy's) sex organs?*

30. *How young were you the first time you ever saw the sex organs of a woman (or man)?*

In recording the responses, the interviewer is interested in noting the respondent's age at the time of the experience and how the experience occurred. For instance, if the respondent accidentally entered a room when a baby's diaper was being changed (recorded as **B** for baby) or if the occurrence happened accidentally, the recording would note **accd** for accident. If the response was peeking, it would be so noted, **pk**.

Example of Responses and Coding

Female, never married, age 51, college graduate (see Figure 12–4)

1. *How young were you the first time there was ever any sex play with other girls?*

   Oh, yes, I remember way back when I was a little girl, there was some.

FIGURE 12-4.   Female

		6=/X	X
		√m 10=/	
		√m 2♀	
		√ 1 Xa	
		X	
		9-11 ¼	1 X@8
		√m 50♂	X
		√m	√=U
		√p	X upset
		X	X tell
		X	
		4B	10 F pk
		1 X@12 nude	
		w Bro	

What grade were you in?

Well, it must have been about the first grade.

You were about six then?

Yes.

How often did it happen?

One time.

All right, what other sex play did you have?

Oh, then there was a girlfriend I had when I was about 10 years old and we used to sleep together, and she was about my age in school.

2. *And how often did you have sex?*

That went on for about a year and it must have been once a week.

So, let's see, you've had experience in early sex play with two girls?

Yes, that's right.

3. *Okay, now, in your sex play, was there showing of sex organs?*

Yes.

4. *Was there touching of sex organs?*

Yes.

Did you show your sex organs?

Yes, and I looked at my partners.

Did you touch your sex organs or touch your partners'?

Yes, they touched mine and I touched theirs.

Then both showing and touching were in both directions?

Yes.

5. *Well, did you put anything into your sex organs like fingers or sticks or anything you might have been playing with?*

Well, one time we did that, and I did it to my partner. As a matter of fact, I put my finger in her vagina.

6. *All right. Did they put their mouth on your sex organs?*

No, we never did that.

7. *Did you put your mouth on their sex organs?*

No.

8. *When was the first time you ever had any sex play with boys?*

Well, there were a bunch of kids in the neighborhood who used to play hide and seek and sometimes we'd get in little corners and play with each other.

Okay. How old were you then?

I was about 9 years old.

9. *How long did you play those kinds of games?*

Oh, I guess we did that from the time I was 9 until—oh, I guess I was about 11 when we stopped.

And how many boys were involved?

Altogether, about five boys, on and off.

And how often did it happen?

Oh, about once a month.

All right. Was there any other sex play with boys?

No, not that I remember.

10. *When you were playing, did you show your genitals to one another?*

Yes, it was dark, but yes, we did that.

11. *And did you touch each other's sex organs?*

Yes, we did that too.

12. *And did you ever put your mouth on any of the boys' sex organs?*

They used to do that to me but I never did it to them.

13. *Was there any insertion of objects into the penis or the urethra of the male sex organ?*

No, we never did that.

14. *Was there ever any insertion into the anus of any of the boys?*

No, not that I remember.

15. *As a child, what sex-play experiences did you have with women older than you?*

Do you mean before I was a teenager?

Yes.

Oh, I never had any experience back then with a grown woman.

22. *Okay. Before you started to menstruate, what experiences did you have with adult males? Say, men who were five years or more older than you?*

Well, I had an experience one time when I was 8, an uncle came and visited with us and he was fooling around, wrestling with me and he put his hand up my dress and touched me down there and I became very upset about it.

Did you tell anybody about it?

No, I was afraid to tell anybody. I didn't like it. I was really upset.

Okay. Was this the only experience you ever had with an adult male as a child?

Yes, that was the only time.

29. *When was the first time you ever saw the sex organs of a baby boy?*

Well, I had a brother who was four years younger than me, so I guess I saw him ever since I was 4 years old.

30. *And when was the first time you ever saw the sex organs of an adult male?*

Well, one time I was peeking at my father in the bathroom. I was curious and wondered what he looked like.

How old were you at the time?

Oh, I guess I was about 10 years old.

BACKGROUND INFORMATION					
HEALTH			DREAMS	INCIDENTAL	
				PROSTITUTION	
				PREMARITAL	CONTRACEPTION
		PRE-		COITAL	
		ADOLESCENT		ATTITUDES	EXTRA-
	EROTIC	SEX PLAY			MARITAL
	AROUSAL				COITUS
MARRIAGE					
			PREMARITAL	FIRST	INCIDENTAL
			PETTING	COITUS	HOMOSEXUALITY
		PUBERTY			
				MARITAL	ANIMAL
	FAMILY			COITUS	CONTACTS
	BACKGROUND				
ANATOMY				PREMARITAL	
		SELF-	RECREATION	COITUS	
		MASTURBATION			OTHER
					SEXUAL
					BEHAVIORS
	SEX				
	EDUCATION				
			GROUP SEX		

FIGURE 13-1

13

Self-Masturbation

The Self-Masturbation block is one of the most important parts of the sex history. We know that masturbation occurs in 96 to 98 percent of all males and 65 to 80 percent of all females, including well over 50 percent of married males and females.

Masturbation information can be particularly helpful in diagnostic evaluations of transsexuals, where frequency of masturbation, techniques, and fantasies play an important role in a differential diagnosis. For others, information about inhibitions, the nature of one's fantasies, and acceptance of one's body are very important.

This information is easy to get from males of upper social levels, who tend to accept masturbation as normal behavior. From lower social level males, however, it is very difficult, and questions about masturbation must be asked later in the sexual history. For females it is generally best not to ask about masturbation as the first major type of sexual behavior. The information will often be easier to elicit after the Premarital Petting and several Coitus blocks have been completed.

Although masturbation does not cause nearly as much concern to people today as it did twenty-five or fifty years ago, there is still a great undercurrent of guilt, repression, uneasiness, and worry about it. Therefore, for preorgasmic women, teaching them to masturbate is usually effective and is one of the techniques most often used in therapeutic intervention. For impotent males and premature ejaculators, dealing with their masturbatory patterns both by themselves and with their partners is very important.

The location of the block is shown in Figure 13-1. The location of responses to the questions is shown in Figure 13-2. The items tapped are:

1. Ages when masturbated; when orgasm reached
2. Learned about through telling and/or reading
3. Learned about through witnessing
4. Learned about by being masturbated

5. Learned through self-discovery	9. Masturbation frequencies
6. Ages when thought it would cause physical harm	10. Current frequencies
	11. Techniques
7. Ages when felt guilt	12. Average length of time to climax
8. Maximum frequency in any one week	13. Fantasies during masturbation

Question 1

How young were you the first time you tried to masturbate yourself?

When did you first have an orgasm in self-masturbation?

Questions 2-5

The next four questions are concerned with how the subject learned about masturbation. There are four possibilities: (1) learning about masturbation by being told or reading about it; (2) learning by seeing others masturbate; (3) learning by being masturbated by someone else; and (4) learning by self-discovery.

Question 6

The following examples of questions are designed as suggestions to help the interviewer focus on whether the respondent ever experienced any of the old fears or myths surrounding masturbation: that it causes insanity, weakens the body, stunts one's growth, uses up semen, causes blindness, etc.

FIGURE 13-2

	1		
	2	*9*	
	3		
	4		
	5		
	6		
	7		
	8		
	10		
	11a	*b*	
	c	*d e*	
	12		
	13		

Did you ever think that masturbation would harm you in any way?

Make you sick?

Stunt your growth?

Affect you physically?

Question 7

Did you ever feel guilty about masturbation?

If the answer is positive, record the ages when the subject felt guilty.

Question 8

What is the maximum number of times in a week you have ever masturbated?

Question 9

How often did you masturbate when you were a child? From ages 11 to 14? Since age 16?

Question 10

How often do you masturbate now?

Question 11

How do you masturbate?

The checklist for female masturbation techniques includes: (a) clitoral stimulation, (b) bed masturbation, (c) anal stimulation, (d) use of objects including fingers for stimulation of any of the genital areas including the vagina, and (e) vibrators. If other methods—e.g., urethral insertions—are used, an asterisk is used to indicate that they are listed at the bottom of the form.

The checklist for male techniques of masturbation includes: (a) manual, (b) bed masturbation, (c) anal stimulation, (d) self-fellation, and (e) use of objects. If the respondent tried but was not able to self-fellate, the attempt is recorded as **try**. If the respondent thought about self-fellating but had not tried it, the response is recorded as **th**.

Question 12

How long does it take you to come to climax in self-masturbation?

The measurement is taken in minutes, recorded as '' **seconds** ', or any way the interviewer can get the information.

Question 13

What do you think about when you masturbate?

A checklist of fantasies might be used: rape, group sex, homosexual, sadomaso-chism, animals, oral-genital sex, intercourse, etc.

Examples of Responses and Coding

A. *Female, married, age 25 (see Figure 13–3)*

1. *You mentioned that sometimes after petting with boys, you would go home and masturbate. How young were you the first time you ever tried to masturbate yourself?*

   Oh, I've been doing that since I was 5 years of age.

   All right. When did you first have an orgasm in self-masturbation?

   Oh, that didn't come along until I was about 11.

2–5. *How did you learn about masturbation?*

   I just found it out for myself. (Coded in fifth line)

   Nobody talked to you about it?

   No.

FIGURE 13-3.   Female

6. *Did you ever think that masturbation would harm you in any way?*

No, I never did.

7. *Ever feel guilty about it?*

There was a time when I was in high school when my gym teacher told me that it would be harmful. Maybe from 14 to 16 I felt a little guilty about it.

8. *What do you suppose is the greatest number of times in one week that you ever masturbated in your life?*

Oh, I should think every day for a week.

9. *All right. Back when you were a child—say, 5 to 11—how frequently did you masturbate?*

Oh, I would guess once a week, maybe.

And from 11 to 14, how often did you masturbate?

It was about the same until I got into high school. Then I cut way back, say twice a year.

All right. And after you were through feeling guilty about it, say after 16, how frequent was masturbation then?

Oh, it went back to about once a week until I was married at 22.

10. *On the average, how often do you masturbate now?*

I would say about once in two weeks.

11. *(a) How do you masturbate?*

Clitoral stimulation.

(b) Have you ever used bed masturbation?

I don't know what you mean.

Have you ever pushed your genitalia against a bed or pillow or a table to masturbate?

No, I've never tried that.

(c) Have you ever used anal stimulation to masturbate?

Oh, once in a while, yes.

(d) Have you used other ways to masturbate? Water for example? Objects?

No, I can't think of any other way.

(e) Have you used a vibrator?

I tried one once but I didn't enjoy it.

12. *About how long does it take you to come to climax in self-masturbation?*

Oh, I usually delay it for ten or fifteen minutes.

13. *What do you think about when you masturbate?*

My husband sometimes.

And what else do you think about?

Oh, other men occasionally.

Do you think about women sometimes?

No, I don't.

About animals?

No.

Ever think about being raped?

Yes, it's funny you mentioned it. I have had those fantasies, but I am always in control of the situation.

Have you ever fantasied bondage? Being held down?

No, I never have.

FIGURE 13-4.   Male

	13-15	
	✓ ¼ (-15)	
	X	
	X	
	X	
	? crzy	
	X	
	2/	
	X	
	✓ X	
	X X X	
	2′	
	♀C X♂	
	X rape	
	X Z′	

B. *Male, never married, high school drop-out, age 20 (see Figure 13–4)*

  1. *How old were you the first time you jacked off?*

Oh back when I was a kid, that's kid stuff.

All right, how old would you guess?

Oh, I guess I shot my load first when I was thirteen.

2–5. *Where did you hear about jacking off?*

Oh, you hear from the other guys, all the time.

Have you actually seen them jack off?

No.

They try to jack you off?

No, I just heard about it.

  6. *Did you ever think it would hurt you in any way?*

Oh, you hear all sorts of stories about that. I was never sure whether it would hurt me or not.

How did you think it would hurt you?

Go crazy.

  7. *Did you feel guilty about it?*

No, I don't have no guilt.

  8. *What is the greatest number of times you ever jacked off in any one week?*

Oh, about two I guess.

  9. *Okay, say back at 13 to 15, how often did you jack off?*

Oh, not very often. If I couldn't get any from the broads, maybe once a month.

And say from 15 until you dropped out of high school at 17, how often?

No, I quit that completely.

And since 17 how often?

Not at all.

 10. *On the average, how often do you masturbate now?*

I don't at all right now.

11. *How would you jack off?*

    With my hand, of course.

    Did you ever lie on the bed and move up and down against your penis?
    No.

    Did you ever stimulate your ass when you jacked off?
    No.

    Would you ever use bottles or tubes, like toilet paper tubes or other objects?
    No, I never did that.

12. *How long would it take you to come?*

    Oh, a long time. Maybe two minutes.

13. *And what did you think about when you jacked off?*

    I thought of having some broad and I wasn't able to get her.

    All right. Would you ever think of men?
    No.

    Ever think of animals?
    No, I never did that.

    Ever think of raping somebody or tying them up, or hurting them?
    No, I never think of that sort of thing.

    Did you think of intercourse itself or would you think of fooling around or petting with a girl?
    No, it was always screwing her.

BACKGROUND INFORMATION

HEALTH			DREAMS		INCIDENTAL PROSTITUTION	
				PREMARITAL COITAL ATTITUDES		CONTRACEPTION
		PRE-ADOLESCENT SEX PLAY			EXTRA-MARITAL COITUS	
	EROTIC AROUSAL					
MARRIAGE						
		PREMARITAL PETTING	FIRST COITUS			INCIDENTAL HOMOSEXUALITY
		PUBERTY				
	FAMILY BACKGROUND				MARITAL COITUS	ANIMAL CONTACTS
ANATOMY			PREMARITAL COITUS			
	SELF-MASTURBATION	RECREATION				OTHER SEXUAL BEHAVIORS
	SEX EDUCATION					
		GROUP SEX				

FIGURE 14-1

14

Dreams

The primary focus of this block is to identify dreams that stimulate orgasm in the respondent. Dreaming to orgasm is one of several possible outlets, as listed under the discussion of Question 2 in the Puberty chapter (Chapter 11). In males they are sometimes called "wet dreams." For females, there are no simple terms to describe the phenomenon, except possibly "dreaming off," so the phrase "dream to orgasm" is used.

The questions in this block can be asked early in the interview as the respondent does not feel responsible for orgasm while sleeping, and the questions therefore do not usually meet with resistance. Most males have little difficulty recognizing wet dreams. Recognition of the comparable experience is much more difficult for females. Short of being awakened by orgasm or of heavy lubrication providing some evidence, many females simply don't realize that dreaming to orgasm has occurred. Some women may continue to sleep through orgasm and may wonder upon awakening whether the orgasm was part of the dream or actually occurred as a result of dreaming. Survey research therefore provides scant data on dreams to orgasm in females. A woman can, however, usually make an educated guess as to whether she dreamed *to* orgasm or *about* orgasm.

Wet dreams in males occur primarily in adolescence, although some men continue having dreams to orgasm until quite late in life. Females tend to have dreams to orgasm later in life rather than during adolescence. The incidence and frequency of dreams to orgasm appear to be higher in upper social level males and females than in lower social level persons.

It is important to obtain information on dreams for at least three reasons: (1) dreams are a fundamental part of a person's sex life; (2) dream content frequently provides clues to a person's overt sexual history; and (3) issues of guilt and concern sometimes become apparent through sex-dream exploration.

The information elicited in this block is as follows:

1. Ages when dreams occurred
2. Frequency
3. Content
4. Nonorgasmic sex dreams

Figure 14–1 shows the location of the block and Figure 14–2, the location of the responses.

The first three questions are concerned with sex dreams to orgasm, and the fourth, with sex dreams not to orgasm. The professional interested in dream analysis may want to develop a more specific explanation of content and a more elaborate method of recording the information.

Question 1

(Male) *How young were you the first time you ever had a wet dream, or had an orgasm while dreaming?*

(Female) *How young were you the first time you ever had an orgasm while dreaming?*

This question is concerned with the respondent's age range of experiencing dreams to orgasm. The most efficient way to get such a range is to identify the first and the most recent occurrences, and then to identify frequencies within that range. If the respondent gives an adolescent age—say, 15 years old—then the interviewer pursues the information by asking:

When was the last time you had one?

FIGURE 14-2

Males, in particular, experience wet dreams around pubescence. If the respondent reports that the last wet dream occurred at 18 years of age, then the range is 15–18, inclusive.

Identifying the upper limit of the age range enables the interviewer to cut corners in the process of establishing the respondent's frequency of dreams to orgasm. Obviously, if a 55-year-old male reports that his last wet dream was experienced before his marriage at age 30, the interviewer need not pursue the frequency of dreams to orgasm during the previous twenty-five years in this respondent's history.

Question 2

How frequently did you have wet dreams from _____ to _____?

    or

Since the first time, how often have you had dreams to orgasm?

Question 2 is concerned with how often the respondent has dreams to orgasm. Rather than pursue an average per year, month, or week, the interviewer tries to get the information by asking for the total number of experiences during the age range, established in the replies to Question 1, when dreams to orgasm are/were experienced.

Question 3

What did you dream about?

It is important to identify the content of wet dreams, especially *recurring* themes in dreams to orgasm. To help pinpoint fantasy material, the interviewer may use the same kind of checklist used in the Masturbation block. For example:

Coitus and oral-genital stimulation
Sadism/masochism
Rape
Sex with animals
Group sex
Bondage/discipline
Explicit sexual behavior: heterosexual, homosexual, bisexual

Question 4

Have you ever had sex dreams when you did not come to orgasm?

What did you dream about?

This is concerned with content of dreams of a specific sexual nature that did not lead to orgasm. Dreams that are highly romanticized, especially dreams of walking down the aisle in a marriage ceremony, having a baby, or being in love with somebody, are not considered sex dreams. A sex dream must include some overt sexual action or activity, such as hugging, kissing, petting, breast stimulation, masturbating, intercourse, etc. Again, the interviewer can explore such material with the respondent by repeating the same checklist used in Question 3. Both frequencies and dream content are recorded.

Examples of Responses and Coding

A. *Male, age 43, college graduate (see Figure 14-3)*

1. *How young were you the first time you had a wet dream?*

   Oh, yes, I've done that, I was 15.

   And when was the last time you had a wet dream?

   I had a few in college. I was about 21, I guess.

2. *All right. From age 15 through high school, say 15 to 18, how frequently did you have wet dreams?*

   Well, not too often. Maybe once a month.

   And in college?

   Oh, there were much fewer then. Maybe the whole time in college, four times.

3. *And what did you dream about?*

   I dreamed about women.

FIGURE 14-3. Male

	15 – 21	
	¼ – 18 4x (-21)	
	♀ CPGO xH	
	♀ CGO $\frac{x z}{s>m}$	
	X grp	

What about women? Did you have intercourse with them?
Oh, sure.

Did you dream about petting with them?
Of course.

How about oral sex?
Yes.

Did you dream about males sometimes?
Never.

Did you have wet dreams that involved animals?
I don't remember any.

Ever any sadistic or masochistic dreams?
A little . . . but more sadistic than masochistic.

Any group sex?
No.

4. *Have you ever had sex dreams where you didn't come?*
Oh, I have a few . . . not very many.

What do you dream about?
Just women. Mostly fucking and some sucking.

Fine.

B. *Female, age 36 (see Figure 14–4)*

1. *How young were you the first time you ever came while dreaming?*
Just recently I started an affair, so I've done that, say, in the last two years.

Well, let's see. You're 36 now, so you started at age 34?
Yes.

Did you ever have any before?
Not that I can remember.

2. *How often do you suppose you have these dreams?*
Oh, maybe six times a year, or something like that.

FIGURE 14-4. Female

	34-d	
	1/8 xGO	
	♂c xH	
	x xSM	
	xz	

3. *What do you dream about?*

I dream about my lover.

What is your lover's gender?

Oh, he's a male.

What are you doing with your lover?

We're having intercourse.

Are you having oral sex?

No, I don't remember dreaming about that.

Are there other females in your sex dreams?

No.

Any animals?

No.

Any sadism or masochism?

No.

4. *Do you sometimes have sex dreams when you don't come?*

I can't remember my dreams very well.

Not anything at all?

No, I'm just blank.

Okay.

BACKGROUND INFORMATION

HEALTH

DREAMS

INCIDENTAL PROSTITUTION

PREMARITAL COITAL ATTITUDES

CONTRACEPTION

PRE-ADOLESCENT SEX PLAY

EXTRA-MARITAL COITUS

EROTIC AROUSAL

MARRIAGE

PREMARITAL PETTING

FIRST COITUS

INCIDENTAL HOMOSEXUALITY

PUBERTY

MARITAL COITUS

ANIMAL CONTACTS

FAMILY BACKGROUND

ANATOMY

PREMARITAL COITUS

SELF-MASTURBATION

RECREATION

OTHER SEXUAL BEHAVIORS

SEX EDUCATION

GROUP SEX

FIGURE 15-1

15

Premarital Petting (Heterosexual)

The information covered in this block includes what the respondent has experienced sexually with both petting partners and intercourse partners before marriage but following puberty. If the person being interviewed has had both petting and premarital intercourse experience, information in the block includes the number of partners with whom the respondent has had petting experiences as well as the number with intercourse experiences. The questions on petting techniques include both petting and intercourse partners. If a respondent has never married, regardless of age, information in this block would include sexual behavior to the time of the interview.

Although petting is known by various names—"necking," "making out," "getting it on," "hot and heavy"—the specific behavior the term denotes to most people in this culture is physical lovemaking activities short of sexual intercourse. It involves such sex-play activities as caressing, kissing, embracing, fondling, stroking—"in a gentle, loving manner," according to Webster. As is apparent in the numerous terms for petting, it is not a fixed set of behaviors or a pattern involving an established set of acts. It is a series of overt behavioral acts ranging from subtle touching to anything short of intercourse.

Usually, however, these behavioral acts follow a predictable progression, and research has identified a sequence of sexual behaviors which is relatively inflexible, from the least intimate behavior such as hugging to the most intimate, such as oral-genital sex. It seems obvious that one experiences lip kissing before deep tongue kissing; kissing is typically experienced before breast stimulation; hand on breast before mouth on breast; breast stimulation before manual genital stimulation; manual stimulation before oral stimulation; etc. This hierarchy of behaviors is not necessarily experienced in the same sequence during each petting encounter. While one person may take weeks, months, or years to progress up the hierarchy, another may telescope all the behavior into a single encounter. The only possible exception to this pattern in the hierarchy is "apposition of nude genitals" occurring *before* oral sex. Apposition of nude genitals is sometimes not part of the hierarchy because it simply does not occur, and if it does occur, it often precedes experience with oral-genital sex. Apposition as a petting technique usually occurs with relatively inhibited or very young people.

Although this block is called Premarital Petting, the block can be divided into vertical columns to accommodate petting after divorce and extramarital petting, depending on the sexual experiences of the respondent.

The location of the Premarital Petting block is shown in Figure 15-1. The eighteen questions asked in this block are listed below, with the location of responses shown in Figure 15-2.

1. Ages involved
2. Number of different partners to high school graduation
3. Number of different partners from high school graduation to marriage (or to the interview date if never married)
4. Hugging
5. Kissing
6. Tongue kissing
7. Male hand on female breast
8. Male mouth on female breast
9. Male hand on female genitals
10. Female hand on penis
11. Male mouth on female genitals
12. Female mouth on penis
13. Nude apposition of genitalia without penetration
14. Frequency of male orgasm in petting
15. Frequency of female orgasm in petting
16. Reactions to—petting, arousal, tension, jitters
17. Ache in groin
18. Self-masturbation after petting

Question 1

How young were you the first time you experienced hugging or kissing, necking or petting following puberty?

It is important to include all four terms—hugging or kissing, necking or petting—in asking the question, so that there is no misunderstanding about the information being sought. Remember that the response must *not* include experiences prior to puberty. Party games or casual goodnight kisses are not included.

Usually when a person begins to have petting experiences, he or she will continue the activity with some regularity until marriage or the time of the interview. If the interviewer knows that the respondent is not married and the response to the first-time question was "14," the interviewer might want to assume that the activity has continued to the date of the interview and record **14-d**. If the respondent married at age 22, the appropriate recording would be **14-21**, meaning that premarital petting began at age 14 and continued until marriage at age 22. (The year prior to the respondent's age at marriage is always used to record the information because it is understood in recording a figure that the activity continued through the age recorded.) Another assumption that is made to lessen the burden of mental calculations is that the age at marriage is recorded in round numbers—i.e., assumed to be 22.0 years, disregarding months or weeks into the year.

FIGURE 15-2

	1	
	2	
	3	
	4	
	5	
	6	
	7	
	8	
	9	
	10	
	11	
	12	
	13	
	14	
	15	
	16	
	17	
	18	

Question 2

Up until high school graduation, with how many different partners was there any hugging or kissing, necking or petting?

Question 3

From high school graduation until marriage (or to the present), with how many different partners was there any hugging or kissing, necking or petting?

If the respondent replies with the common response, "I can't possibly remember," the interviewer provides choices that fall well outside the range of the respondent's possible experience.

Was it 2 or 3, 500, 15, 75, 7?

As noted earlier, the interviewer proposes a wide range to encourage the person to come up with a reasonable answer. For example, if the interviewer asks: "Was it 2 or 3, 15 or 50?" the response is likely to be "50," even if the correct number is 75, but if the interviewer asks, "Was it more like 20 or 3, 15 or 500?" the response is likely to be, "Oh my, no! It was only 75."

At this point, the interviewer has a choice to make. If he or she is convinced that the respondent has experience in premarital coitus (usually the interviewer will have little difficulty determining this), the interviewer may decide to skip the remainder of this block and go directly to the primary question of the First Coitus block:

How young were you the first time you had intercourse?

If the response is "after marriage," it is recorded in the First Coitus block and the interviewer may return to the Petting block questions.

If the response is a dubious "some time in high school or college," the interviewer asks,

How many people did you have intercourse with before marriage?

If the response is "15," then the interviewer must return to the petting column and confront the respondent by explaining:

Now, you told me there were fifteen people you necked or petted with. Are those the same people you had intercourse with?

The respondent might reply,

Oh, some of them are, and some of them aren't.

Then the interviewer must further ask:

How many of these fifteen people you petted with did you not have intercourse with?

Oh, there were only five of those.

The coding for this response would be **5 + 15C**.

If the respondent says he or she had coitus with twenty-five people before marriage, the next question is:

Did you include these twenty-five partners with the fifty with whom you petted?

If the response is yes, an alternate form of recording is **50 inc 25C**. If the response is no, the recording is **50 + 25C**. Recording an **X** means there were no partners with whom the respondent experienced petting.

Questions 4 through 13 are petting technique questions. They include partners with whom the respondent has had intercourse as well as partners with whom only petting has been experienced, and are concerned with a hierarchy of petting techniques, from hugging to apposition of nude genitalia with penetration.

In presenting the questions, the interviewer initially adopts a tone of "telling" the respondent rather than "asking," in the following checklist manner:

Now, let's see, there was hugging? Kissing? Tongue kissing?

Note that the questions are objectified by using the "there was" phrasing. Using this checklist rather than asking the respondent what techniques were used ensures that the interviewer will obtain a more complete profile of the respondent's techniques and minimizes any embarrassment the respondent might feel if forced to verbalize erotic behavior.

Responses may be recorded using the check system or, depending on individual research needs and interest, more elaborate documentation of information may be necessary. For instance, for some purposes, especially therapy, it is important to know whether "mouth on genitalia" is coded a minus, − , or a check, ✔.

As the interviewer progresses down the list of techniques, his or her tone might change to one of "asking" as opposed to "telling," depending on the respondent's apparent comfort or discomfort and the interviewer's perception of the subject's willingness to respond. Thus the questioning might continue,

Did you put your hand on your partner's genitalia?

The following listing provides appropriate phrasing for each question for both male and female respondents:

4. *There was hugging?*

5. *There was kissing?*

6. *There was tongue kissing?*

7. (male respondent)

   You put your hand on your partner's breast?

   (female respondent)

   There were his hands on your breasts?

8. (male respondent)

   You put your mouth on your female partner's breast?

(female respondent)

Your partner put his mouth on your breast?

9. *There was hand on female genitalia?*

10. *There was female hand on penis?*

11. *There was mouth on female genitalia?*

12. *There was mouth on penis?*

13. (upper social level)

Was there ever lying together with nude genitalia touching without having intercourse?

(lower social level)

Was there ever dry fucking with naked sex organs together?

If a subject appears to have had a wide range of petting experience, the interviewer may decide not to ask the upper part of the hierarchy of behavior (Questions 4–10) but to begin with "mouth on genitalia" (Question 11 or 12). If the response to this question is negative, the interviewer backtracks to the less intimate question of "hand on genitalia" (Question 9 or 10). This skipping is done less often with lower social level persons, who may be inhibited about using a variety of petting techniques —or talking about them.

Questions 14 and 15 are concerned with frequency of orgasm in petting and are divided to allow recording of both male and female orgasm. These are the questions asked for a male respondent:

Question 14

How young were you the first time you came to orgasm in petting without intercourse?

Question 15

How frequently did your partner come to orgasm without intercourse?
(Use check system to record.)

These are asked of a female respondent:

Question 15

How often did your partner come to orgasm in petting without intercourse?

Question 14

How young were you the first time you came to orgasm in petting without intercourse?

Note that in taking a female history, the interviewer asks Question 15 before asking Question 14 because most women seem to find it easier to answer questions about what was done to them.

Question 16-18

These questions get at any after-effects as a result of petting.

16. *Did petting sometimes leave you tense, nervous, jittery, or unsatisfied?*

Using the word "sometimes" gives the respondent the flexibility to answer in degrees, as very rarely, frequently, etc. Recording is done with checks.

Question 17 is concerned with aches in the groin as a result of petting. Groin and pubic area aches are sometimes called by males "stone aches," "lover's nuts," or "hot nuts," but it is also important to ask female respondents about such aches after petting, as they experience them as frequently as males do.

The question asked is as follows (male respondent):

17. *After petting, did you ever have an ache in the groin or sex organs?*

(female respondent)

After petting, did you ever have an ache in the sex organs or pelvic area?

Question 18 asks about self-masturbation resulting from petting. This question frequently provides an easy lead-in for the female respondent to reveal self-masturbation. The question asked is:

18. *Did you ever masturbate after petting?*

Example of Responses and Coding

Male, married at age 25 (see Figure 15-3)

1. *How young were you the first time you experienced any hugging or kissing, necking or petting after puberty?*

   I was 14.

2. *From age 14 until high school graduation, with how many different females was there hugging or kissing, necking or petting?*

   Quite a few. I can't remember exactly.

   But approximately; was it more like 5, 300, 25, 800?

   Oh, about 50.

3. *From high school graduation until marriage, with how many different partners was there any hugging or kissing, necking or petting?*

   Approximately 100.

Fine.

How old were you the first time you had intercourse?
16.

Up until high school graduation, how many different females did you have intercourse with?
Three.

From high school graduation to marriage, with how many females was there intercourse?
Twenty.

FIGURE 15-3.   Male

	14-24	
	50+3C	
	100 inc 20 C	
	✓	
	✓	
	✓	
	✓	
	±	
	✓	
	−	
	4 ♀	
	X	
	±	
	15-18 ½ 18-24=	
	? 42x	
	✓	
	3x	
	X	

Are these twenty included in the 100 with whom there was petting?
Yes.

4. *There was hugging?*
   Yes.

5. *There was kissing?*
   Yes.

6. *There was tongue kissing?*
   Yes.

7. *Hand on female breast?*
   Yes.

8. *Mouth on female breast?*
   Sometimes, not always.

9. *Hand on female sex organ?*
   Yes.

10. *Female hand on penis?*
    Very seldom.

11. *Mouth on female sex organ?*
    With only four women.

12. *Female mouth on penis?*
    No.

13. *Was there ever any lying together with nude sex organs touching?*
    It happened a few times.

14. *How old were you the first time you came in petting without intercourse?*
    15.

    From 15 to high school graduation, how often did you come in petting without intercourse?
    About once in two weeks.

    From 18 until marriage, how often did you come in petting without intercourse?
    About six times a year.

15. *Did the females have orgasm in petting?*
I don't know.

16. *After petting, would you sometimes feel nervous, tense, jittery?*
Oh, very frequently.

17. *Would you ever be left with a stone ache?*
I can remember that happening about three times.

18. *Would you go home and masturbate after petting?*
No.

BACKGROUND INFORMATION

HEALTH			DREAMS		INCIDENTAL PROSTITUTION	
		PRE-ADOLESCENT SEX PLAY		PREMARITAL COITAL ATTITUDES		CONTRACEPTION
	EROTIC AROUSAL				EXTRA-MARITAL COITUS	
MARRIAGE			PREMARITAL PETTING	FIRST COITUS		INCIDENTAL HOMOSEXUALITY
		PUBERTY				
	FAMILY BACKGROUND				MARITAL COITUS	ANIMAL CONTACTS
ANATOMY		SELF-MASTURBATION	RECREATION	PREMARITAL COITUS		OTHER SEXUAL BEHAVIORS
	SEX EDUCATION		GROUP SEX			

FIGURE 16-1

16

First Coitus

This block elicits a description of the first sexual experience with penetration of the penis in the vagina. The definition must be made clear. If the response is "My first sexual intercourse experience was when I was 15, but I was impotent," it is not considered a first coital experience since no penetration occurred.

First coitus can be very traumatic and is a well-remembered experience for most people. An entire block has been given to first intercourse because our society makes such a big point of it. This is when a woman "loses her virginity." Our society does not usually consider it a "loss" when a male has intercourse for the first time but often a triumph.

This block deals only with postpubertal coitus. Sexual dysfunctions such as impotence, premature ejaculation, vaginismus, and dyspareunia frequently have their basis in this first experience. For well-educated males, questions about first intercourse are usually asked after the Masturbation and Premarital Petting blocks are completed. For less-educated males, however, First Coitus is the first block asked after Puberty is established because it is the best-accepted sexual activity, and it is socially sanctioned. Because our society does not freely grant permission to the female to have intercourse, for females First Coitus is usually not asked until after the Petting block is completed, but it is usually asked before the Masturbation block.

The location of the First Coitus block is shown in Figure 16–1. The information elicited in this block is listed below and recorded as indicated in Figure 16–2.

1. Age at first intercourse
2. Partner (companion or prostitute)
3. Age of partner
4. Male's enjoyment
5. Female's enjoyment
6. Time after marriage before first intercourse

FIGURE 16-2

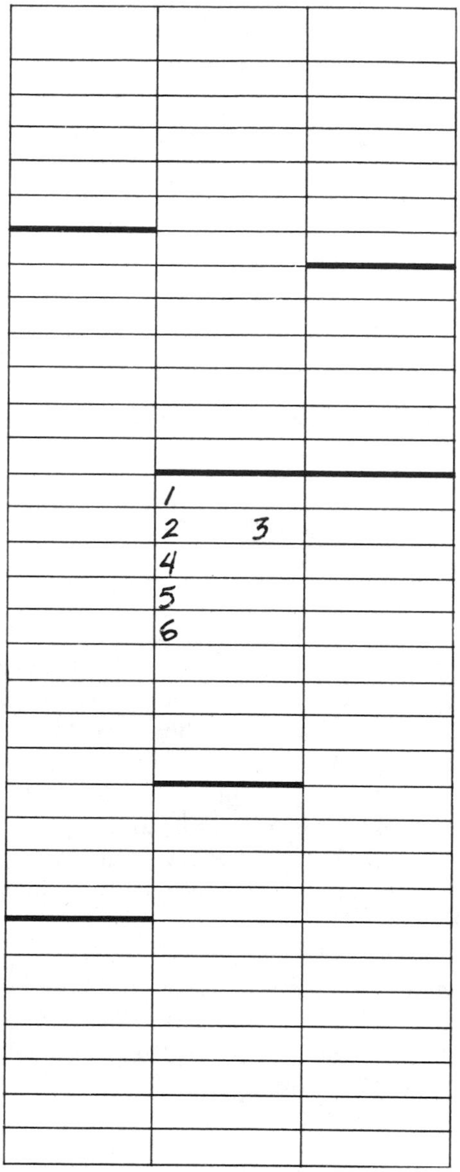

Question 1

How old were you the first time you had intercourse?

Question 2

Was your partner a companion or a prostitute?

This question is generally not asked of a woman, since very few females have first intercourse with a male prostitute.

Question 3

How old was your first partner?

Question 4

Did you enjoy your first sexual experience? Describe it.

The check system may be used:

⌐   very satisfying

X   disastrous

It is useful here to write in descriptive words for enjoyment or lack of enjoyment. The entire story can be recorded at the bottom of the page if the interviewer feels it is important.

Question 5

Did your partner enjoy the experience?

Question 6

How long after your first marriage did you have your first sexual intercourse?

If the interviewee is not married, this question is not asked. We are concerned only with intercourse in first marriage and with reasons for a delay, such as vaginismus, fear, anxiety, or impotence. It is assumed that there will be less difficulty in subsequent marriages. If the respondent had premarital intercourse with his or her spouse this question need not be asked because it can be assumed that they will have had intercourse right after marriage.

Examples of Responses and Coding

A. *Male, grade-school-educated laborer, age 50, married at 18 (see Figure 16–3)*

  1. *How old were you the first time you fucked?*

     I was 14 years old.

FIGURE 16-3. Male

	14	
	C = 25	
	✓	
	✓?	
	# 1	

2. *Was your partner a companion or a prostitute?*

She was the neighborhood lay.

Did you pay her?

Naw.

3. *How old was your partner the first time you had sexual intercourse?*

She was old. Probably 25.

4. *Did you enjoy your first sexual intercourse?*

Yeah, it was great.

FIGURE 16-4.   Female

	21	
	C = 24	
	✓? ✓	
	−INDIF·HI ✗	
	#2 tired	

5. *Did your partner enjoy your first sexual intercourse experience?*
Yeah. I guess so.

6. *How long after your first marriage did you have your first sexual intercourse?*
Right away. A few hours after the wedding.

Fine.

B. *Female, college-educated, 34 years old, married at age 30 (see Figure 16–4)*

1. *How old were you the first time you had sexual intercourse?*

I was 21.

Fine.

Question 2 is generally not asked of a woman, since very few females have first intercourse with a male prostitute.

3. *How old was your partner the first time you had sexual intercourse?*

He was 24.

O.K.

4. *Did your partner enjoy your first sexual experience?*

Orgastic?

I really don't know. I suppose he did. I know that he came.

5. *Did you enjoy your first sexual experience?*

Did you have an orgasm?

Describe it.

I got high at a party and I found myself in a bedroom with a man who insisted on intercourse. I was indifferent. I did not have an orgasm.

6. *How long after your (first) marriage did you have your first sexual intercourse?*

We drove to the airport after the wedding and flew to Paris. When we got there we were very tired, too tired for sex, so we went to sleep. So I guess you might say it was the next evening, about twenty-four hours later.

BACKGROUND INFORMATION

HEALTH			DREAMS		INCIDENTAL PROSTITUTION	
				PREMARITAL COITAL ATTITUDES		CONTRACEPTION
		PRE-ADOLESCENT SEX PLAY			EXTRA-MARITAL COITUS	
	EROTIC AROUSAL					
MARRIAGE						
			PREMARITAL PETTING	FIRST COITUS		INCIDENTAL HOMOSEXUALITY
		PUBERTY				
	FAMILY BACKGROUND				MARITAL COITUS	ANIMAL CONTACTS
ANATOMY				PREMARITAL COITUS		
		SELF-MASTURBATION	RECREATION			OTHER SEXUAL BEHAVIORS
	SEX EDUCATION					
			GROUP SEX			

FIGURE 17-1

17

Premarital Intercourse

In our society today, it is common to hear people talking about "sex before marriage" as though it were synonymous with premarital intercourse. Obviously everyone has "sex before marriage," but not everyone has premarital intercourse. As an outcome of the so-called sexual revolution, more people have premarital intercourse than was true in past eras, and the attitude toward these premarital sexual relationships seems to be slowly changing in the direction of acceptance. We are also seeing the phenomenon of more couples (and groups) living together openly in a sexual relationship outside marriage. This change is not revolutionary; it it evolutionary.

Through the ages, the emphasis on the unbroken hymen has raised questions and concerns that are still significant today. The exalted importance of virginity, combined with the double standard which permits and even encourages the male to have premarital intercourse while it punishes the female for the same behavior, is still very much in evidence in modern Western society.

It is essential to obtain a complete history of premarital intercourse from each respondent, including descriptions of partners, frequencies, and techniques—first, because this is an important part of everyone's sexual history and, second, because it often exposes feelings of guilt, inhibition, and fear that need to be understood if the respondent is a candidate for treatment.

Figure 17-1 shows the location of the Premarital Intercourse block. The information elicited, recorded as indicated in Figure 17–2, is as follows:

1. Time lapse between first coitus and the first orgasm (females only)

2. Percent of the time subject had orgasm in premarital intercourse (females only)

3. Age range during premarital intercourse
4. Frequencies
5. Number of partners
6. Number of prostitutes
7. Frequency of intercourse with spouse before marriage
8. Oldest partner's age
9. Respondent's age at the time
10. Youngest partner's age
11. Respondent's age at the time
12. Age preference in partners
13. Number of partners who were virgins
14. Number of married partners
15. Nearest relative subject had intercourse with
16. Ages of female at premarital pregnancies
17. Age of male when female became pregnant
18. Outcome of pregnancies
19. Feelings associated with pregnancies

Questions 1 and 2 (asked only of females)

1. *How long after your first intercourse did you have your first orgasm during intercourse?*

2. *Before marriage, about how often did you have an orgasm during intercourse?*

FIGURE 17-2

Question 3

At what ages did you have premarital intercourse?

Question 4

Before marriage, about how often were you having intercourse?

Question 5

About how many different sexual partners did you have before marriage?

Question 6

Were your sexual partners companions or prostitutes?

This question is usually omitted when interviewing a female. It is assumed that all partners were companions.

Question 7

About how often did you have intercourse with your spouse before marriage?

Questions 2 through 7 are omitted for respondents who were never married. If the respondent is currently married, it may be easier to ask the questions in the Extramarital Coitus block before asking Questions 8 through 19 in this block because the Extramarital Coitus block will give background information and introduce the subject matter for the rest of this block.

Question 8

What was the age of the oldest partner you ever had intercourse with?

Question 9

How old were you then?

Question 10

What was the age of the youngest partner you ever had intercourse with?

Question 11

How old were you then?

Question 12

What do you consider the ideal age for a sexual partner for you now?

Question 13

How many of your partners in intercourse were virgins before they had intercourse with you?

Question 14

How many of your sex partners were married and living with their spouses when they had intercourse with you?

Question 15

Who is the closest relative you ever had intercourse with?

Incest is certainly one of the taboo subjects, and the suggested phrasing of Question 15 seems to be the gentlest and easiest way to inquire into the matter. If the respondent shows surprise, the interviewer may ask, "Was it a cousin? an uncle? or some other relative who is not as close as a parent?" Of course, if the respondent indicates a positive response, the interviewer needs to explore incest with other relatives.

Question 16

(Males) *How many women did you impregnate before marriage? How old were they at the time?*

(Females) *How many premarital pregnancies did you have? How old were you at the time?*

Question 17

(Males) *How old were you at the time?*

(Females) *How old was the father at the time?*

Question 18

What was the outcome of the pregnancy?

If there was more than one pregnancy, lines 16 through 19 can be divided vertically and responses recorded for each.

Question 19

How did you feel about the outcome?

Examples of Responses and Coding

A. *Female, age 26, college-educated, married at age 22 (see Figure 17-3)*

1. *You told me that you had your first intercourse at 16, and that you didn't particularly enjoy it. How long after your first intercourse until you had your first orgasm during intercourse?*

   Oh, it was about a year.

FIGURE 17-3.   Female

2. *Before marriage, what percentage of the time did you have an orgasm during intercourse?*

I would say about half.

3. *What were your ages when you were having premarital intercourse?*

Well, from 16 until now I have had intercourse continually.

4. *All right. From 16 to 18, about how often were you having intercourse with males?*

About once in two weeks.

And from 18 until you were married at 22, how often?

Oh, I would say then it was once or twice a week.

5. *How many different men do you suppose you had intercourse with from 16 to 22?*

I would judge about ten different men.

7. *You told me you knew your husband about six months before marriage. How often were you having intercourse with him before you were married?*

About once or twice a week.

For the entire time?

No, for only the last four months.

If the respondent has never married, proceed with the questions in order. If the respondent is currently married, it may be easier to ask the questions in the Extra-marital Coitus block before asking Questions 8 through 19 in this block because that block will give background information and introduce the subject matter for the rest of this block.

8. *All right, now take all the men you had intercourse with in your life. What is the age of the oldest man you ever had intercourse with?*

He was 45 years old.

9. *And how old were you then?*

That was last year.

You were 25.

Right.

10. *And the youngest man you ever had intercourse with?*

Well, he was 17.

11. *And how old were you then?*

    I was 16.

12. *If you were to have intercourse now with a male and consider only age, what age male would you prefer?*

    or

    If you had males lined up from age 6 to 106, what age male would you prefer to have intercourse with?

    Well, I would take someone a little older than me.

    About how much older?

    Oh, I would say about 30.

13. *How many men have you had intercourse with who had never had intercourse until they had it with you? How many were virgins?*

    I can think of only one.

14. *How many men were married and living with their wives when they had intercourse with you?*

    I can only think of three.

15. *Who is the nearest relative you ever had intercourse with?*

    Well, as I told you before, when I was very young I used to play around with my brother, but we never really had intercourse.

    All right, but after you started menstruating, what sexual contact with relatives did you have?

    None.

16. *How many times were you pregnant before you were married?*

    I was pregnant one time.

    How old were you?

    I was 21.

17. *How old was the male when you were pregnant?*

    That was my husband, and it was three months before we got married.

18. *What was the outcome of the pregnancy?*

    I had an abortion.

19. *And how did you feel about that?*

    We were both much relieved.

B. *Male, age 55, married from age 24 to age 30; divorced since age 30 (see Figure 17-4)*

3,4. *You told me that you first had intercourse when you were 14. Now, from 14 until you finished high school, how often were you having intercourse?*

I was getting it every chance I could.

How often was that?

I would say at least three times a week.

And from 18 until you were married at 24, how often were you having intercourse?

Six times a week.

5. *Not counting prostitutes, how many different women do you think you had intercourse with before you were married?*

I couldn't begin to count them up.

Well, let's make a guess. In high school, how many do you think?

Oh, at least 100.

FIGURE 17-4. Male. The vertical line indicates the two pregnancies.

And from 18 to 24?
There had to be at least 300 more.

So that makes 400 different women?
That's right.

6. *When was the first time you ever paid a women for intercourse?*
   I suppose at 18. (Put **18** on line 1 of Incidental Prostitution block.)

   How many prostitutes did you have intercourse with before marriage?
   Not very many, maybe 35. (This is recorded on line 6 in this block.)

7. *How often did you have intercourse with your wife before you were married?*
   Never. I married a virgin. She had it the first time on our honeymoon.

8. *What is the age of the oldest woman you ever had intercourse with?*
   About 60.

9. *And how old were you?*
   That was two years ago. I was 53.

10. *How old was the youngest female you ever had intercourse with?*
    That was back in high school, and she was 13.

11. *How old were you?*
    I was 14.

    O.K.

12. *What age woman do you like to have intercourse with now?*
    I don't have any preference.

    If you had them all lined up from 6 to 106, which would you take?
    I'd take them one at a time. I have absolutely no preference, one is as good as the other.

13. *How many virgins have you had intercourse with?*
    At least a dozen.

14. *How many women were married and living with their husbands when you had intercourse with them?*
    About 100.

15. *Who is the nearest relative you ever had intercourse with?*

    I had intercourse with my sister. I was 14 and she was 13.

    How often did you have intercourse with her?

    Maybe six or eight times.

    Did you ever get caught?

    No, it was one of those passing things.

    What other relatives have you had intercourse with?

    Well, when I was 22, I had intercourse with an aunt who was 45. I just happened to be visiting her and we had intercourse one time.

16. *How many women did you knock up before you were married?*

    I can remember at least two. At least they claimed I was the father.

    [The vertical line in Figure 17–4 indicates the two pregnancies.]

17. *And how old were you when this happened?*

    The first time I was 18; the second time I was 20.

    How old were the women?

    The first was 17 and the other about 30.

18. *What happened with the pregnancies?*

    I really don't know. They got rid of it some way, I don't know how.

19. *How did you feel about this?*

    This is their business, their problem, and they need to take care of it themselves.

BACKGROUND INFORMATION

HEALTH			DREAMS		INCIDENTAL PROSTITUTION	
				PREMARITAL COITAL		CONTRACEPTION
		PRE-ADOLESCENT		ATTITUDES	EXTRA-MARITAL COITUS	
	EROTIC AROUSAL	SEX PLAY				
MARRIAGE						
			PREMARITAL PETTING	FIRST COITUS		INCIDENTAL HOMOSEXUALITY
		PUBERTY				
	FAMILY BACKGROUND				MARITAL COITUS	ANIMAL CONTACTS
ANATOMY				PREMARITAL COITUS		
		SELF-MASTURBATION	RECREATION			OTHER SEXUAL BEHAVIORS
	SEX EDUCATION					
			GROUP SEX			

FIGURE 18-1

18

Incidental Prostitution

Prostitution is defined as accepting money payment specifically for sexual relations—i.e., intercourse, mouth-genital stimulation, anal intercourse, and sexual play involving sadomasochism, group sex, bondage, and discipline, etc. It does not include situations in which nonmonetary gifts, goods, or services are provided for each sexual encounter, nor when expenses are paid for. "Incidental prostitution" means experience with fewer than six partners, and for less than three months. If the respondent's experience exceeds these limits, the separate prostitution inventory (Chapter 30) is used.

The four types of prostitution include heterosexual relations for which the partner, whether female or male, is paid, and homosexual prostitution, both female and male. The information in this block is concerned with heterosexual prostitution only. Lines 1 through 5 refer to the subject as being the payer, line 6 refers to the subject as the payee. Questions about male homosexual prostitution and the rare occasions of female homosexual prostitution are asked in a separate homosexual inventory (Chapter 29).

Experience with prostitution can be anything from a single encounter to years of experience. The Kinsey researchers reported that 69 percent of the total white male population had had some experience with prostitution.* Familiarity with possible motivations for the use of a prostitute's service may help an interviewer in identifying clues for the behavior described by respondents:

1. Activity with nonprostitutes may not be available elsewhere, and intercourse with a prostitute may be the most readily available sexual outlet.

*A. C. Kinsey, W. B. Pomeroy, and C.E. Martin, *Sexual Behavior in the Human Male* (Philadelphia; W. B. Saunders, 1948), Table 138, p. 598; Figure 153, p. 599.

2. Prostitution provides partner variety.
3. Organized prostitution, as in a house, may provide less risk of veneral disease than contact with streetwalkers and nonprostitutes.
4. Prostitution provides an arena for the curious who like to experiment.
5. Peer pressure in groups sometimes motivates people, especially men, to participate in prostitution.
6. Prostitution is often less expensive than dates with companions who are wined and dined and entertained with no guarantee of intercourse being accomplished.
7. Prostitution allows the participant to avoid involvement, commitment, and responsibility as is not necessarily true of sexual involvement with nonprostitute partners, where involvement is quite frequently on a social and legal basis.
8. Prostitution frequently provides a variety of sexual techniques and activities not available elsewhere, such as mouth-genital stimulation, sadomasochism, fetishes, group sex, voyeurism, and exhibitionism.
9. Prostitution is a source of sexual outlet for people who are ineffective in forming relationships with others, especially the handicapped, deaf, blind, severely crippled, or physically deformed.

Although there are fewer males today who have their first premarital intercourse experience with prostitutes, it remains a source of sexual activity for many. Because there is far more incidental prostitution than might be believed, this block is an important area to cover in taking a sexual history. The last line of this block asks whether the respondent has ever been *paid* by the opposite sex for sexual activity. For heterosexual males, this is quite rare but must nonetheless be asked.

The location of the Incidental Prostitution block is shown in Figure 18-1. The items elicited are listed below, and the location of the responses is shown in Figure 18-2.

1. Ages experienced
2. Frequency
3. Number of partners and ages
4. Money paid
5. Techniques used
6. Has the respondent ever been paid

Question 1

In taking a male history, Question 1 is:

At what age did you first pay a female for sexual activity?

The extraordinarily low incidence of male prostitution with heterosexual females suggests that a basic assumption of relatively limited experience is appropriate. Thus, the question to females is phrased:

Have you ever paid a male for intercourse?

All ages of involvement are recorded here, including premarital, extramarital, and postmarital experiences.

FIGURE 18-2

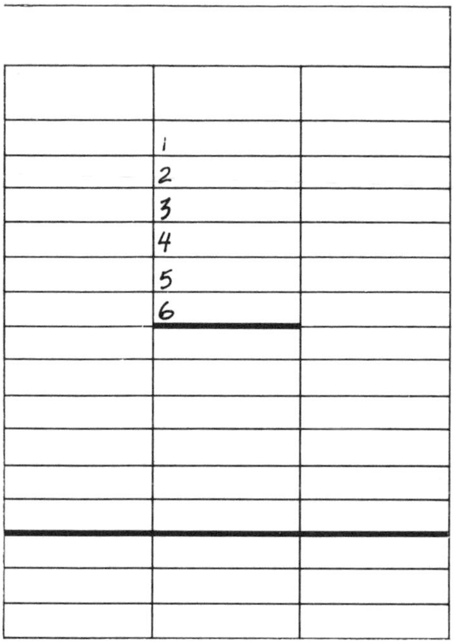

Question 2

The concern here is with the frequency with which the respondent has paid a prostitute for sexual activity.

The phrasing of this question will depend on the respondent's answer to Question 1 regarding age of first experience with prostitutes. For instance, if a respondent has had limited exposure, the interviewer may ask the exact number of times intercourse with prostitutes was experienced. If the respondent reports an age range for experience with prostitutes, then the frequency of coitus may be recorded in averages per week, month, or year. For those with limited experience, the question asked is:

How often have you paid for intercourse?

For those with a wide range of experience, information on frequency is broken into age or experience segments and the questions, asked separately, are;

At age _____, how often did you pay . . . ?

    or

Between ages _____ and _____, how often did you pay . . . ?

Question 3

This is concerned with total number of prostitutes with whom the respondent has had paid intercourse. The prostitutes' ages or age range is also recorded. The questions, asked separately, are,

What is the total number of different partners with whom you've had paid intercourse?

and

What are their ages?

Question 4

How much did you pay for intercourse?

Question 5

What techniques were used during your experience with prostitutes?

The interviewer may wish to use the checklist of techniques in Premarital Petting (Chapter 15), or Self-Masturbation (Chapter 13) to aid the respondent in identifying specific experiences.

Question 6

This is concerned with whether the respondent has ever been paid for intercourse.
    If the interviewer suspects the respondent has had limited experience with prostitution, then the question asked is:

Have you ever been paid for intercourse?

    If the interviewer suspects that the respondent may have experience with prostitution, the question would be:

How young were you the first time you were paid for intercourse?

Examples of Responses and Coding

A. *Male, age 42, married at age 25 (see Figure 18–3)*

  1. *How young were you the first time you ever paid a female for intercourse?*

     I was just 19.

FIGURE 18-3. Male

	19-28	
	10×(19-25) 3×(26-28)	
	8 = 18-29	
	50 1= 15	
	GO√C√ An·Mp = 1×	
	X	

And when was the last time you paid a female for intercourse?

When I was 28.

O.K.

2. *Before you were married, say from 19 to age 25, how often did you pay females for intercourse?*

Well, not very often, maybe a total of ten times.

And since your marriage, from ages 26 to 28, how often?

It was only three times then.

And you've had no intercourse with prostitutes since the age of 28?

That's right.

O.K.

3. *What is the total number of different females you've paid for intercourse?*

There have been a total of 8.

O.K. What were their ages?

I don't know for sure, but they were young.

What would you say was the age of the youngest?

She looked to be about 18.

And how old do you think the oldest one was at the time you had intercourse with her?

She was probably around 29.

Good.

4. *How much did you pay the women for intercourse?*

Well, all of them had different prices.

What was the least amount you ever paid?

I never paid less than $15, nor more than $50.

On the average, what did it cost you?

Come to think about it, all but one of the girls were call girls, and they mostly charged $50.

All right.

5. *What techniques were used during paid intercourse?*

Mostly I was interested in a blow job.

Fine. Was there intercourse too?

Yes, we did that too.

What other things did you do?

I tried anal sex a couple of times, and once a pro jerked me off.

Were there any other techniques that you remember?

No, that's all I ever did.

O.K. Fine.

6. *Have you ever been paid for intercourse?*

No, I never have.

B. *Female, age 54, divorced at age 39 (see Figure 18–4)*

1. *Have you ever paid a male for intercourse?*

Yes, I have.

FIGURE 18-4. Female

	43-53	
	2/m(45-49)2x(-53)	
	3=23·?26·28	
	I=100 I=50 I=35	
	C·√GO xAn =Ix	
	Ix 40/bar	

How young were you the first time you ever paid a male for intercourse?
I was 43.

And when was the last time you paid a man?
Just last year.

O.K.

2. *Between the ages of 43 to 53, how often did you pay for intercourse?*
Oh, I used such services quite regularly.

How regularly would you say?
I can't really remember precisely.

Was it every week, or twice a year, or once a month?
I started with one gentlemen on a regular basis for the first six years.

How regularly did you see him during that period?
I saw him about twice a month.

Did you pay anyone else for intercourse during those first six years, say from age 43 to 49?
No, he was the extent of my interest.

And from age 49 to 53, how often did you pay for coitus?

Oh, that's easy. I only saw two other men I paid, each one one time only.

Then you paid for intercourse approximately 146 times, that is twice a month for six years is 144 plus the two single experiences?

I didn't realize it was that much, but the calculations are correct.

3. *What is the total number of different males you've paid for intercourse?*

Well, there was my regular partner of six years and then two others.

That's right. What were their ages?

Now?

No, at the time you were having intercourse with them.

Let's see. One was 28, one was about 23 and the other I'm guessing was probably somewhere in between, maybe around 26.

O.K.

4. *How much did you pay the men for intercourse?*

You mean including gifts?

I mean cash on the barrelhead each time you had intercourse.

My regular man was always $100. And the other two were less.

How much were they?

One was $50 and the other about $35.

Great.

5. *What techniques did you use?*

Oh, we just had sex.

You mean intercourse?

Yes.

Was there any mouth genital contact?

No. I never allowed that.

Was there any anal intercourse?

Once, but we always had straight sex.

Fine.

6. *Have you ever been paid for intercourse?*

Well, it's funny that you should ask. One time I was in a singles bar, and a man insisted on paying me $40 for intercourse, which I would've been happy to have had without payment, but he went ahead and paid me.

What other times?

That was the only time.

C. *Seaman, age 35, married from age 23 to age 26, lived wandering life (see Figure 18–5)*

1. *How young were you the first time you paid a woman for intercourse?*

16.

2. *All right. From 16 until you were married at 23, how often did you pay a woman for intercourse?*

I guess it averaged once a week.

And during your marriage, how often did you pay a woman for intercourse?

It was only about once in two weeks.

And since the break-up of your marriage at 26 to now, how frequently have you paid a woman for intercourse?

I would estimate two to three times a week.

FIGURE 18-5. Seaman

3. *Can you make any rough guess as to how many different women you have paid for intercourse? Remember, we're talking only about the ones you've paid.*

    Oh, it would be impossible for me to estimate the number.

    Well, let's do a little arithmetic. From 16 to 23 is about seven years, averaging once a week which means about fifty times a year or about 350 times. How many women do you think that would mean?

    It was usually a different woman every time. Maybe 300 different women.

    All right. And during your three years of marriage, you were paying about twenty-five times a year or about seventy-five times.

    Yes, that would probably mean fifty different women.

    And from 26 to 35, which is about nine years, at maybe 125 times a year or maybe upwards of 1000 times.

    Yes, I guess when you put it that way, the total number of women would be close to 1,500 women.

4. *How much do you usually pay for intercourse?*

    Well, it varies a lot, but I suppose it would average $10 per trick, although it's ranged all the way from $2 to $35.

5. *All right, now what did you do sexually with the women you paid?*

    Everything.

    Intercourse?

    Yes.

    Would they go down on you sometimes?

    Oh, once in a while.

    Would there be anal intercourse?

    No, they never let me do that.

    Would they give you a trip around the world?

    That's happened three times.

    Has there been group sex?

    No, never.

6. *Has a woman ever paid you for intercourse?*

    Yes, I remember once a woman had hot pants and I met her in a bar and she slipped me $5 to fuck her.

BACKGROUND INFORMATION						
HEALTH			DREAMS		INCIDENTAL	
					PROSTITUTION	
				PREMARITAL		CONTRACEPTION
		PRE-		COITAL		
		ADOLESCENT		ATTITUDES	EXTRA-	
	EROTIC	SEX PLAY			MARITAL	
	AROUSAL				COITUS	
MARRIAGE						
			PREMARITAL	FIRST		INCIDENTAL
			PETTING	COITUS		HOMOSEXUALITY
		PUBERTY				
					MARITAL	ANIMAL
	FAMILY				COITUS	CONTACTS
	BACKGROUND					
ANATOMY				PREMARITAL		
		SELF-	RECREATION	COITUS		
		MASTURBATION				OTHER
						SEXUAL
						BEHAVIORS
	SEX					
	EDUCATION					
			GROUP SEX			

FIGURE 19-1

19
Premarital Coital Attitudes

Although the inventory described on these pages focuses primarily on sexual behavior rather than attitudes, because of the continued prevalence of pejorative attitudes toward premarital intercourse, this block includes a group of questions concerned with attitude development as it affects behavior. The questions have to do with why the respondent did not have any or did not have more premarital intercourse. This information can be helpful in getting at moral restraints, inhibitions, and conformity or nonconformity in all groups. Also included is information on attitudes about marriage.

Figure 19-1 shows the location of the block in relation to other blocks and Figure 19-2, the location of responses to the following questions:

1. Moral restraint
2. Fear of pregnancy
3. Fear of VD
4. Public opinion
5. Scarcity of opportunities
6. Lack of interest
7. Wanted marriage
8. Wanted children, and how many
9. Wanted to marry virgin
10. Was spouse a virgin

Questions 1-6

The first six questions concern the respondent's reasons for not having premarital intercourse, or for not having more than he or she has had. Although some of the reasons are practical in nature (e.g., fear of VD or of pregnancy), this block was de-

FIGURE 19-2

	1	2	
	3	4	
	5	6	
	7	8	
	9	10	

veloped to identify specific attitudes which influence a person's involvement in overt sexual behavior.

The deterrents most frequently mentioned relate to issues of morality, fear of pregnancy or sexually transmitted diseases, public opinion, and the degree of the individual's interest and opportunity. Questions 1 through 6 list these concerns.

Although the six restraints are listed individually and all should eventually be posed to the respondent, the questions are not asked in order. The interviewer's concern is primarily with why the person has not had any (or more) intercourse prior to marriage. To get information from a respondent on personal inhibitions against engaging in sexual intercourse, the interviewer may need to ask several leading questions before identifying the restraints in the inventory—for example, "Why do you think you haven't?" Such questions help the respondent (1) by serving as a prod to encourage him or her to sort out personal feelings about a specific behavior, and (2) by preventing the respondent from evading the issue by offering ambiguous or defensive responses to the questions about premarital coitus, ("I don't know," "I can't remember"). The question may be asked in either the past or the present tense, depending on the respondent's experience with intercourse:

What kept you from having premarital intercourse?

or

What are the factors that held you back from having more intercourse?

This question is always asked, regardless of the respondent's experience with intercourse. For example, many interviewers might assume that a respondent reporting a high frequency of coitus has had "enough" whereas the respondent may feel that he or she did not have intercourse as often as he or she would have liked. In the process of discussing the respondent's attitudes toward premarital intercourse, the interviewer can facilitate easy identification of specific attitudes by using all six restraints in checklist fashion, asking each question (in either past or present tense) by suggesting them as possibilities; for example, "Was it because of fear of pregnancy?" or "Was it because of lack of interest?"

Questions 7-10

These questions are concerned with attitudes about getting married, having children, and male and female virginity.

Question 7

If the respondent was never married, the question asked is:

Do you want to get married?

If the respondent is currently or has been married, the question is:

When you got married, did you want to get married?

If the respondent has been married more than once, the interviewer may want to record responses to the question for each of the marriages and can do so by numbering the marriages and coding the response beside each number.

Some of the reasons people marry include pressure from partners or parents or peers, a need to be taken care of, the death of a parent(s), the desire for companionship, the wish to move out of the family house, the need for security, and others.

Question 8

If the respondent has never married, the question is:

When you get married, will you want children, and how many?

If the respondent is or has been married, the question is:

Did you want children?

If the response is affirmative, the follow-up question is:

How many did you want at the time you got married?

Again, in the case of a respondent with multiple marriages, the interviewer may choose to record responses to this question individually for each marriage.

Question 9

For never-married respondents, the question asked is:

When you get married, will you prefer to marry a virgin, a nonvirgin, or does it make no difference to you?

For married or formerly married respondents, the question is:

When you got married, did you want to marry a virgin, a nonvirgin, or didn't it make any difference to you?

Question 10

This question is concerned with the respondent's *perception* of partner/spouse virginity. For never-married respondents, the question is:

Do you think your marital partner will be a virgin?

For currently and previously married respondents, the question is:

At the time of marriage, was your spouse a virgin?

Recording information for Questions 7 through 10 may be accomplished by using the check system and abbreviating specific response information. For Question 9, "a virgin" is coded as **V**, "a nonvirgin" is an **X**, and "it doesn't make any difference" is coded as = . Combinations of responses, such as "It didn't make too much difference, but if I really had to choose, I think I would have preferred a virgin," can be coded as = **V**.

Examples of Responses and Coding

A. *Female, virgin, age 18, unmarried (see Figure 19–3)*

Why haven't you had intercourse?

Oh, I'm really not sure.

Why do you think you haven't?

I guess I'm not really old enough.

Why aren't you old enough?

I'd die if my parents found out, and I don't think my boyfriend would really respect me.

FIGURE 19-3.   Female

4. *Would you say, then, that you have a fear of what other people would think of you?*

Yes, especially my friends and family.

1. *Are there moral issues that prevent you from having intercourse?*

Yes, I'm concerned about being a good Catholic and living up to my religious upbringing.

2. *Would you say that the possibility of pregnancy prevents you from having intercourse?*

Oh my goodness, no!

In recording, "X" (✓) here means that the respondent says she does not regard fear of pregnancy as a personal deterrent to premarital intercourse (her answer is recorded in quotes), but something that she said—"I'm saving pregnancy for marriage"—suggests to the interviewer that fear of pregnancy may be part of the reason for this person's restraint. This is recorded as [✓] to indicate that the interviewer's perception differs from the respondent's answer.

3. *Does the fear of possibly contracting a sexually transmitted disease, like gonorrhea, deter you?*

No, I've never really thought about that.

6. *Are you at all interested in having intercourse?*

Yes, I've given it a lot of thought.

5. *Are there opportunities for having intercourse?*

There certainly are. Most everywhere.

7. *Do you want to get married?*

Oh, I'm looking forward to it!

8. *Will you want children?*

Yes, I'm interested in having a family.

How many children will you want to have?

Probably three or four.

9. *When you marry, will you prefer to marry a virgin, a nonvirgin, or will this make no difference to you?*

I'd like to think it doesn't make any difference, but I really prefer a nonvirgin.

For any particular reason?

He's got to know more than I.

O.K.

In this case, to ask Question 10 concerning partner as virgin would be superfluous, as this respondent has never had an intercourse partner.

B. *Experienced male, age 42, married (see Figure 19–4)*

Why didn't you have more premarital intercourse?

Unless you went to prostitutes, there weren't all that many women who were doing it when I was single. At least not that I knew.

1. *Did you not have more for any moral reasons?*

No.

2. *Did a fear of making the women pregnant prevent you?*

I don't think so.

FIGURE 19-4. Male

	X X		
	X X		
	✓ X		
	— ✓=1 ♂		
	♂ >♀ exp ✓?		

3. *How about fear of getting VD?*

   No.

4. *Were you concerned about what people might think?*

   You mean if they found out I was doing it.

   Yes.

   It was to my advantage to have everybody know!

6. *Was there a lack of interest in having more sex?*

   I was interested, I just couldn't find enough partners.

7. *When you got married, did you want to get married?*

   Yeah, I sorta wanted to get married, but I didn't know her long enough.

8. *Did you want children?*

   Yes, I was very interested in kids.

At the time you got married, how many children did you want?

I was only interested in having a son.

So you only wanted to have one child?

Yes.

9. *When you got married, did you want to marry a virgin, a nonvirgin, or didn't it make any difference?*

I wanted a virgin.

Do you remember why?

Sure, I wanted to be sure I was more experienced than her.

10. *At the time of marriage, was your spouse a virgin?*

I assume so! But I really don't know. We never discussed it.

That's just fine.

In recording, ✓♂ > ♀ **exp.** indicates that the respondent wanted to marry a virgin so that he would have more experience than she. A recorded response of ✓? means that the respondent thinks his spouse was a virgin at the time of marriage but doesn't know.

BACKGROUND INFORMATION

HEALTH			DREAMS		INCIDENTAL PROSTITUTION	
				PREMARITAL COITAL ATTITUDES		CONTRACEPTION
		PRE-ADOLESCENT SEX PLAY			EXTRA-MARITAL COITUS	
	EROTIC AROUSAL					
MARRIAGE						
			PREMARITAL PETTING	FIRST COITUS		INCIDENTAL HOMOSEXUALITY
		PUBERTY				
	FAMILY BACKGROUND				MARITAL COITUS	ANIMAL CONTACTS
ANATOMY				PREMARITAL COITUS		
		SELF-MASTURBATION	RECREATION			OTHER SEXUAL BEHAVIORS
	SEX EDUCATION					
			GROUP SEX			

FIGURE 20-1

20
Marital Coitus

In the early phase of marriage, intercourse is usually very frequent. This period may last from a few days to six months. Frequency usually becomes routinized after that. In most marriages, however, frequency gradually declines.

If the frequency and techniques of intercourse become routine, this may lead to sexual apathy or dysfunction. The interviewer looks for a sudden break or pattern change, such as a marked increase or decrease in activity, and asks the respondent, "What happened?" Such pattern changes can be clues to illness, apathy, depression, or extramarital relationships.

Preferred petting techniques and positions often provide clues to the respondent's attitudes toward sexual behavior. Patterns of restraining and inhibiting behaviors or of freedom and relaxation probably show up more clearly in the sexual relationship with the spouse than anywhere else in the interview.

The location of the Marital Coitus block is indicated in Figure 20-1, and that of the responses to the following items is shown in Figure 20-2:

1. Frequency
2. Maximum frequency in any seven-day period
3. Duration of foreplay
4. Kiss
5. Tongue kiss
6. Hand on breast
7. Mouth on breast
8. Hand on female genitals
9. Hand on male genitals
10. Mouth on female genitals
11. Mouth on penis
12. Time it takes male to ejaculate after penetration
13. Multiple orgasms in men
14. Male above
15. Female above
16. On side facing partner
17. Sitting
18. Rear entry into vagina

19. Standing
20. Frequency of female orgasm in intercourse and petting
21. Anal intercourse
22. Coitus during menstruation
23. Oral-genital contact during menstruation
24. Have coitus in light or dark
25. Prefer coitus with light on

Question 1

During the first year or two of your marriage, how often did you and your spouse have intercourse?

FIGURE 20-2

	1	
	2	
	3	
	4	
	5	
	6	
	7	
	8	
	9	
	10	
	11	
	12	
	13	
	14	
	15	
	16	
	17	
	18	
	19	
	20	
	21	
	22	
	23	
	24	
	25	

Question 2

What was the maximum number of times you had intercourse with your spouse in any seven-day period?

Question 3

About how much time, on the average, do you spend in foreplay before intercourse begins?

Questions 4 through 11 concern techniques of foreplay and are asked in check-list fashion.

Question 4

There is kissing?

Question 5

Tongue kissing?

Question 6

(Male) hand on (female) breast?

Question 7

(Male) mouth on (female) breast?

Question 8

(Male) hand on female genitalia?

Question 9

(Female) hand on penis?

Question 10

Mouth on female genitalia?

Question 11

Mouth on penis?

Question 12

On the average, how long does it take you (male respondent) *or your husband* (female respondent) *to ejaculate after penetration?*

Question 13

Do you (male respondent) *or does your husband* (female respondent) *ever have more than one orgasm without removing the penis from the vagina?*

There is some confusion about multiple orgasms in the male. Multiple orgasms in the male occur when a second orgasm takes place within twenty minutes of the first one during continuous intercourse (penis in vagina). (A second, or a third or fourth, orgasm does not necessarily mean ejaculation.) There may be a considerable loss of erection, but the intercourse must be continuous to count as multiple orgasms.

Questions 14 through 19 concern positions during intercourse and are asked in checklist fashion.

Question 14

What positions do you use in sexual intercourse? Male above?

Question 15

Female above?

Question 16

On side facing each other?

Question 17

Sitting?

Question 18

Rear entry of vagina (doggie fashion)?

Question 19

Standing?

Question 20

What percentage of the time do you (female respondent) *or does your wife* (male respondent) *have orgasm in intercourse?*

Note that this question relates specifically to orgasm in intercourse (penis in vagina) rather than in petting.

How often do you or does your wife have orgasm during petting?

Question 21

How often have you had anal intercourse?

Question 22

How often do you have intercourse during menstruation? How do you feel about it?

Question 23

How often do you have oral-genital contact during menstruation? How do you feel about it?

Question 24

Do you have intercourse in the light or dark?

Question 25

Which do you prefer?

Example of Responses and Coding

Male, age 35, married at age 25 (see Figure 20-3)

1. *For the first year of your marriage, how often did you and your spouse have intercourse?*

At first often—four times a week at least.

FIGURE 20-3. Male

	4/2 d '/	
	20 /	
	15'	
	✓	
	—	
	✓	
	✓	
	✓	
	✓	
	—	
	±	
	15'	
	1(-2)	
	✓	
	✓	
	—	
	1-2x	
	x	
	x try	
	C = 20% P=50%	
	10x	
	✓ ✓enjoy	
	2/y - Hsb ✓wnt	
	✓	
	✓	

In the past year or two, how often did you have intercourse with your spouse?

About once a week.

Was there a gradual decrease in frequency or was there a sudden drop?

No, it was gradual.

2. *What was the maximum number of times you had intercourse in any seven-day period, including the honeymoon?*

That would be my honeymoon—we really spent three days in bed—

How many times did you have intercourse?

Four times a day for those three days and twice a day after that.

Four times a day for three days and two times a day for four days—that would be twenty times.

Yes.

3. *What is the average time you spend in sex play before intercourse begins?*

I don't watch the clock.

How long do you think it is?

Sometimes not long enough.

30 seconds? 4 hours? 5 minutes? Half an hour? 2 minutes? 2 hours?

I guess about fifteen minutes.

4. *There is kissing?*

Yes.

5. *Tongue kissing?*

Rarely.

6. *Hand on breast?*

Yes.

7. *Mouth on breast?*

Yes.

8. *Hand on female genitalia?*

Yes.

9. *Hand on penis?*

Yes.

10. *There is mouth on female genitalia?*

Rarely.

11. *There is mouth on penis?*

Sometimes.

12. *On the average, how long does it take you to ejaculate after penetration?*

I can really hold back—fifteen minutes.

13. *Do you ever have more than one orgasm in the same continuous intercourse?*
Rarely I will have two.

That means without taking the penis out of the vagina?
Yes.

14. *What positions do you use in sexual intercourse? Male above?*
Yes.

15. *Female above?*
Yes.

16. *On side facing each other?*
Rarely.

17. *Sitting?*
Once or twice.

18. *Rear entry of vagina?*
No.

19. *Standing?*
We tried it but it didn't work.

20. *What percentage of the time does your wife have orgasm in intercourse?*
20 percent.

During petting?
50 percent.

All right.

21. *How often have you had anal intercourse?*
About ten times.

22. *How often do you have intercourse during menstruation?*
I always do.

How do you feel about it?
I especially enjoy it. I seem very aroused at that time.

23. *How often do you have oral-genital contact during menstruation?*
    I like it but my wife isn't too interested.

    How often would you say?
    Twice a year.

24. *Do you have intercourse in the light or dark?*
    Light.

25. *Do you prefer it in the light or dark?*
    In the light.

BACKGROUND INFORMATION						
HEALTH			DREAMS		INCIDENTAL PROSTITUTION	
				PREMARITAL COITAL ATTITUDES		CONTRACEPTION
		PRE-ADOLESCENT SEX PLAY			EXTRA-MARITAL COITUS	
	EROTIC AROUSAL					
MARRIAGE						
			PREMARITAL PETTING	FIRST COITUS		INCIDENTAL HOMOSEXUALITY
		PUBERTY				
	FAMILY BACKGROUND				MARITAL COITUS	ANIMAL CONTACTS
ANATOMY				PREMARITAL COITUS		
		SELF-MASTURBATION	RECREATION			OTHER SEXUAL BEHAVIORS
	SEX EDUCATION					
			GROUP SEX			

FIGURE 21-1

21

Extramarital Coitus

The questions about extramarital sex are asked of respondents who are living together as husband and wife, whether or not they are legally married. Obviously, the block is skipped for other subjects.

Because the inventory asks for a great many particulars about the respondent's sex life, in order to get a total picture it is often necessary to condense some sections and explore only the highlights, returning if necessary to elicit details of extramarital intercourse after the framework has been established. These can be noted at the bottom of the page. For example, suppose a person had extramarital intercourse for ten years with twenty partners at an average rate of once a week. With nineteen of those partners he or she had intercourse only once plus a five-year relationship with one person. If the interviewer is particularly interested in extramarital intercourse he or she may have to develop a special history for this behavior.

Figure 21-1 shows the location of this block in relation to the other blocks.

The following information is elicited and recorded on the lines indicated in Figure 21-2:

1. Age at time of first extramarital intercourse
2. Frequencies
3. Number of partners and their ages
4. Does the spouse know
5. If respondent has not had extramarital intercourse, does he or she expect to have it
6. Has spouse had extramarital intercourse

FIGURE 21-2

	1	
	2	
	3	
	4	
	5	
	6	

Question 1

After your marriage, how old were you the first time you had intercourse with some-one other than your spouse.?

Question 2

How frequently have you had extramarital intercourse?

Question 3

How many partners have you had?

What were their ages at the time?

Question 4

Does your spouse know about your extramarital intercourse?

Question 5

Do you expect to have extramarital intercourse some day?

Obviously, if the answer to Question 1 is "I have never had extramarital intercourse," Questions 2 through 4 are omitted. If the answer is positive, Question 5 is omitted.

Question 6

Do you think your spouse has had extramarital intercourse?

Example of Responses and Coding

Female, college-educated, age 45, married at age 25 (see Figure 21-3)

1. *After your marriage, how old were you the first time you had intercourse with someone other than your husband?*

   It was five years after I was married.

   You were married at 25, so that would make you 30?

   Yes.

FIGURE 21-3. Female

2. *From 30 until you moved to Toledo, how frequent was extramarital intercourse?*

Once or twice a week.

From 38 until now, how frequent?

Not at all.

(Questions 1 and 2 have been combined and the "Peg System," using a place where she lived to aid her recall, is used.)

3. *How many partners have you had?*

I had five partners.

4. *Fine. What were their ages?*

They ranged from 35 to 50.

4. *Does your spouse know about your extramarital intercourse?*

No, but he suspects.

6. *Has your husband had extramarital intercourse?*

I'm not too sure, but I think so—I just have a hunch.

BACKGROUND INFORMATION

HEALTH			DREAMS		INCIDENTAL PROSTITUTION	
				PREMARITAL COITAL ATTITUDES		CONTRACEPTION
		PRE-ADOLESCENT SEX PLAY			EXTRA-MARITAL COITUS	
	EROTIC AROUSAL					
MARRIAGE						
			PREMARITAL PETTING	FIRST COITUS		INCIDENTAL HOMOSEXUALITY
		PUBERTY				
					MARITAL COITUS	ANIMAL CONTACTS
	FAMILY BACKGROUND					
ANATOMY				PREMARITAL COITUS		
		SELF-MASTURBATION	RECREATION			OTHER SEXUAL BEHAVIORS
	SEX EDUCATION					
			GROUP SEX			

FIGURE 22-1

22

Contraception

The development of an individual's sexual pattern includes the history of his or her use of methods for conception control. Sometimes the use of contraception causes considerable conflict in people's lives, for all sorts of reasons. For example, it is not uncommon for young unmarried people to resist the use of contraception because they think it gives the message that they anticipated having intercourse. Such people feel that intercourse should only occur spontaneously. Much of this kind of resistance to contraceptives reflects a denial of personal responsibility for one's sexual behavior and its outcome.

Among the factors that have been found to predict effective use of contraceptives in the United States are increased maturity, high educational level, and high socioeconomic status; additional factors that affect the choice of a particular contraceptive method are race and religion.

The Contraception block's placement on the recording sheet is shown in Figure 22-1, and the questions cover the topics listed below. Figure 22-2 shows the position of the recorded responses.

1. Condoms
2. Diaphragm
3. Spermicidal foam/gel
4. Douche
5. Coitus interruptus
6. Rhythm
7. Intrauterine device (IUD)
8. Female pill
9. Tubal ligation
10. Hysterectomy
11. Vasectomy
12. Other methods
13. Number of pregnancies rated on three options
14. Result of each pregnancy
15. Satisfaction with and effectiveness of contraceptive method

FIGURE 22-2

	1	2
	3	4
	5	6
	7	8
	9	10
	11	12
	13	
	14	
	15	

Questions 1-8

The first eight items are concerned with the use of methods of contraception other than surgical procedures. The question is:

What method of contraception has been used?

For those methods of contraception not immediately identified by the respondent in answering this open-ended question, a checklist of the remaining techniques is used. The check system is used, ✓ for often, ± for sometimes, – for rarely, and **X** for never, to record frequency.

Questions 9-12

Questions 9–11 identify surgical procedures that are used for conception control. Females are asked whether there was a tubal ligation or hysterectomy, followed by their age when it was performed (Questions 9 and 10). Males are asked whether there was a vasectomy and the age when it was done (Question 11). Item 12 can be used to record such procedures as the morning-after pill, ovariectomy, saline preparation abortion, hysterotomy, etc.

Alternate phrasing of questions concerning the use of contraceptive methods are "Do you use . . . ," "Have you ever used . . . ," "How frequently do you use . . . ," "Does your partner . . . ," "Have you ever . . . ," "Has your partner ever . . . ," etc.

Although the inventory is primarily interested in the respondent's use of conception control methods, it is also concerned with contraceptive experiences the respondent has had with partners. As a result, all of the methods listed in the block are asked of everyone, and only the phrasing of certain questions changes depending on individual circumstances and on whether the respondent is male or female. For instance, in asking a respondent about an IUD and a vasectomy, the appropriate questions to ask might be:

	Female Respondent	*Male Respondent*
IUD question:	*Have you ever used an IUD?*	*Has your partner ever used an IUD for protection in intercourse with you?*
		How many of your partners used IUD's while in intercourse with you?
Vasectomy question:	*Does your partner have a vasectomy?*	*Do you have a vasectomy?*
	How many of your partners have had vasectomies?	

Current contraceptive use will be immediately volunteered by respondents when asked, "What kind of contraception do you use?" All of the remaining methods should be explored to determine the extent of each respondent's experience with them and also to provide some crosscheck on frequency of intercourse as recorded in the Premarital, Marital, Postmarital (widowed or divorced), and Extramarital Coitus blocks.

ADDITIONAL SPECIAL CODING INSTRUCTIONS

Any of the methods listed in this block can be used during intercourse on occasions or in periods in a person's life experience that can be categorized by marital status (premarital, marital, postmarital, or extramarital). For instance, rubber condoms are generally used premaritally, except for those individuals who use condoms as protection against sexually transmitted diseases.

Whether a particular type of contraception was used as identified by marital status is then recorded using the following code:

premarital	**Cpm**	(premarital coitus)
marital	**Cm**	(marital coitus)
postmarital	**Cd**	(divorced or widowed coitus)
extramarital	**Cx**	(extramarital coitus)

More than one marital status category may be appropriate for each method, necessitating multiple recordings per line. For example, if a respondent had experience with condom protection both premaritally and extramaritally, the appropriate recording for the condom method would be **Cpm Cx**.

A 39-year-old divorced woman might give the following contraceptive history:

What contraception has been used in the intercourse you have had?

Well, now I use an IUD but I used a diaphragm when I was married.

And before marriage?

Mostly rubbers, but also a diaphragm just before marriage.

Ever use foam or gels?

No.

Ever use douche alone for contraception?

No.

Did the male ever pull out before he came?

Oh, a few times before marriage.

Ever rhythm method?

No.

Ever the pill?

No.

RECORDING OF RESPONSES

1. ✓ **Cpm**   2. ✓ **Cm − Cpm**
3. **X**   4. **X**
5. **− Cpm**   6. **X**
7. ✓ **Cd**   8. **X**

Questions 13-15

These items are concerned with the outcome of any pregnancies the respondent has had (or, if the respondent is a male, any pregnancy he has caused), and with the respondent's attitudes about the effectiveness of the contraceptive method used and personal satisfaction with it.

Questions 13 and 14 are concerned with whether pregnancies, both live births and terminated pregnancies, were planned or unplanned and their outcome. Question 13 asks female respondents:

Were your pregnancies planned?

Males might be asked:

Were your wife's (partner's) pregnancies planned?

The three possible responses to Question 13 are:

1. Planned pregnancy
2. Pregnancy due to failure of contraceptive protection
3. Unplanned pregnancy, i.e., a result of intercourse with no contraception ("carelessness")

A typical answer might be:

Well, our first child was an accident but the last two were planned.

Was the first pregnancy because of failure of contraception?
Carelessness.

This response would be recorded as:

1 = care   2 + 3 = plan

All pregnancies are coded individually according to respondent's age at time of pregnancy with the reason for the pregnancy. For example, a woman reporting one abortion and two live births at ages 16, 20, and 24, respectively, may report that the first pregnancy was due to a condom breaking, the second was the result of unprotected intercourse, and the third was planned. The coding would be as follows:

13. **16 = 2   20 = 3   24 = 1**

The second number in each case refers to one of the three possible causes listed above.

The outcome of pregnancies would be coded as:

14. **1 = abort   2 = ♀ 3 = ♂**

Question 15 asks how satisfied the respondent is with the contraception used and how effective its use has been.

FIGURE 22-3. Female

	√f Cpm √Gn
	X X
	IX >preg X
	X √erM
	X X
	X X
	22=2 24-1
	I=ab 2=♂
	-safe

Example of Responses and Recording

Female, age 30, married, high school graduate (see Figure 22–3)

What sort of contraception do you use?

I use a diaphragm now.

Before your marriage, what were you using?

Well, back when I was in high school, the boys used condoms.

All right, and then what did you use after that, before marriage?

In college I finally went on the pill.

7. *Have you ever used an IUD?*

No, I haven't.

6. *Have you used the rhythm method?*

I'm not sure I know what that means.

That means that you only have intercourse at certain times of the month, when you're not fertile.

No, I've never used that method.

12. *Have you ever used withdrawal—pulling the penis out before ejaculation?*

Yes, we tried that once when I was 22 and I got pregnant.

(Also record the age of first pregnancy on the appropriate line for Question 13 and code the cause of the pregnancy as **2** [see responses to Question 13, below], contraceptive method failure)

Have you ever used jellies or foam?

No, I haven't.

4. *Have you used a douche alone for conception control?*

No, I haven't done that either.

(In this case, it is obvious, since the respondent reports current use of a diaphragm, that her partner has not had a vasectomy and that she has not had a tubal ligation or hysterectomy. Items 9 through 11 are therefore recorded **X**.)

13. *Now you told me about your first pregnancy. Were there any other pregnancies?*

Yes, a second pregnancy that was planned.

How old were you then?

I was 24.

14. *What happened to your first pregnancy?*

I had an abortion.

And the second?

I had my son.

Were there any other pregnancies?

No.

15. *Are you satisfied with the contraception you use?*

Not really, but it's the only one I feel safe with.

BACKGROUND INFORMATION

HEALTH			DREAMS		INCIDENTAL PROSTITUTION	
	EROTIC AROUSAL	PRE-ADOLESCENT SEX PLAY		PREMARITAL COITAL ATTITUDES	EXTRA-MARITAL COITUS	CONTRACEPTION
MARRIAGE			PREMARITAL PETTING	FIRST COITUS		INCIDENTAL HOMOSEXUALITY
		PUBERTY				
	FAMILY BACKGROUND				MARITAL COITUS	ANIMAL CONTACTS
ANATOMY		SELF-MASTURBATION	RECREATION	PREMARITAL COITUS		OTHER SEXUAL BEHAVIORS
	SEX EDUCATION		GROUP SEX			

FIGURE 23-1

23

Erotic Arousal

Questions in the Erotic Arousal block are constructed to identify in very specific ways the kinds of stimulation the respondent finds sexually arousing and those that are not "turn-ons."

It is often difficult for people to determine what erotic arousal is. When asked, "Are you aroused sexually by thinking of another person," the response may be, "Well, how do I know whether I'm aroused or not? What do you mean by being aroused?"

The following operational definition of erotic arousal can provide the clarity needed for responding: "Is there awareness of bodily change such as deep breathing, warm skin, rapid pulse, lubrication (female) or erection (male)?" It is not necessary to have all of these responses to qualify for arousal, but at least some of them will be apparent to the person being interviewed. This description usually satisfies most people, and they know immediately what is meant by sexual arousal.

Erotic arousal information is important to acquire. It identifies another area of sexual behavior in which professionals are interested; it often gives clues to homosexual versus heterosexual behavior or interest; and it gives some idea of the respondent's level of response. (Some people are very quickly, very often, very easily aroused, while others do not have a very low arousal threshhold.)

The information sought in this block (see Figure 23–1 for placement) is listed below and recorded as shown in Figure 23–2.

1. (a) Thinking of opposite sex
   (b) Thinking of same sex
2. (a) Seeing opposite sex
   (b) Seeing same sex
3. (a) Pornographic pictures or art
   —opposite sex
   (b) Pornographic pictures or art
   —same sex

4. Seeing people in overt sex activity in photos or pictures
5. Seeing live sex shows
6. X-rated movies
7. Romantic love stories
8. Music
9. Motion
10. Alcohol
11. Scents, smells, odors
12. Use of mood-altering drugs:
    (a) marijuana
    (b) hashish
    (c) cocaine
    (d) amyl nitrite
13. Drug-use effects
14. Seeing self nude
15. Seeing genitals in self-masturbation
16. Seeing opposite sex nude
17. Seeing same sex nude
18. Seeing erect penis
19. Seeing nude female breasts
20. Seeing male buttocks
21. Seeing female buttocks
22. Do you bite, nibble, scratch, hit, etc.
23. Are you bitten, nibbled, scratched, hit, etc.
24. Reading stories of rape, torture, etc.
25. Animal contact

FIGURE 23-2

	1a b	
	2a b	
	3a b	
	4 5	
	6	
	7 8	
	9 10	
	11	
	12a	
	b	
	c	
	d	
	13	
	14 15	
	16 17	
	18 19	
	20 21	
	22 23	
	24	
	25	

Question 1

Questions 1a and 1b are concerned with the respondent's arousal by thinking of someone of (a) the opposite sex and (b) the same sex in a social situation. (A social situation is defined as any situation that is overtly nonerotic.) The question "Does someone of the opposite sex arouse you sexually?" is too oblique. The phrasing of the question is changed according to the gender of the respondent. A male respondent will be asked:

1. *(a)Are you aroused sexually by thinking of females in a social situation?*

    or

    Does it turn you on to think of women?

1. *(b)Are you aroused sexually by thinking of males in a social situation?*

    or

    Do you get hot thinking of men?

    A female respondent is asked:·

1. *(a) Are you aroused sexually by thinking of males in a social situation?*

    or

    Does it make you hot and bothered to think of men?

1. *(b) Are you aroused sexually by thinking of females in a social situation?*

    or

    Do you get hot thinking of women?

Question 2

Questions 2a and 2b concern arousal caused by seeing rather than thinking of someone of both the opposite and the same sex in a social situation. Again, the phrasing of the question is contingent upon the gender of the respondent. A male is asked:

2. *(a) Are you aroused sexually by seeing females in a social situation?*

    or

    Are you turned on by seeing women socially?

2. *(b) Are you aroused sexually by seeing males in a social situation?*

A woman is asked the same questions in reverse order.

Question 3

Questions 3a and 3b are concerned with the respondent's sexual arousal as a result of seeing nude photographs of (a) opposite sex and (b) same sex in which there is no sexual action.

As in Questions 1 and 2, the order of the questions depends on whether the subject is male or female. A female may be asked:

3. *(a) Are you aroused sexually by seeing pictures or photographs of nude males who are not engaged in sexual activity?*

    or

Does it make you hot to see pictures of naked males?

3. *(b) Are you aroused sexually by seeing pictures or photographs of nude females who are not engaged in sexual activity?*

    or

Does it make you hot to see pictures of naked females?

Questions 4 through 15 are not dependent on the respondent's gender.

Question 4

Question 4 is concerned with the respondent's arousal by sexually explicit photographs or pictures:

Are you aroused sexually by seeing people in photographs or pictures in sexual action?

Questions 5 and 6

Question 5 asks if the respondent is erotically aroused by watching live sex shows, as in night club acts and burlesque. Question 6 concerns arousal by sexually explicit motion pictures. (An operational definition of an X-rated movie is one that people under the age of eighteen years are not allowed to view; further, it shows some sort of specific sexual action, not just nudity.) It is interesting that although an X-rated film usually shows much more overt sexual behavior than a live show, many people find the erotic quality of a filmed performance less stimulating. Questions 5 and 6 are:

5. *Are you aroused by seeing live sex shows?*

6. *Are you aroused sexually by seeing X-rated movies?*

Question 7

Question 7 asks whether the respondent is aroused by reading romantic love stories. This question is important to ask because some people, particularly females, are more aroused by romantic or generalized discussions of sex than they are by the more explicit presentations in X-rated films. Romanticized sex might describe, for example, a dashing knight on a white stallion capturing a fair maiden and swooping her away to be loved and cared for happily ever after. The question is:

Are you aroused sexually by reading romantic love stories?

Question 8

Question 8 concerns the respondent's sexual response to music. Interestingly, the piece of music most often cited as sexually arousing is Ravel's famous crescendo-decrescendo, "Bolero," which was deliberately composed to arouse erotically. Also frequently cited is a selection that builds to climax in the same delibrate way, the "Liebestod" from Wagner's *Tristan und Isolde*. Respondents also frequently cite Tchaikovsky and Bach, rock, disco, and rhythm and blues as erotically arousing music. The question asked is:

Are you aroused sexually by listening to music?

If the answer is affirmative, then an additional question might be asked:

What kind of music do you find most arousing?

Question 9

Question 9 seeks to discover if the respondent experiences erotic arousal as a result of motion, which is defined as any movement that shakes the body even in subtle ways—for example, horseback riding, bicycling, motorcycling, flying, sailing, riding in an automobile, bus, or train. The question is phrased:

Are you aroused sexually by motion?

Question 10

Question 10 addresses the effect of alcohol consumption on sexual arousal. The question is included in the inventory to investigate the belief that alcohol lessens inhibitions rather than arousing eroticism, as respondents typically report. The question asked is:

Does alcohol arouse you sexually?

Question 11

Question 11 seeks to identify any particular scents or smells that may be erotically arousing. The interviewer asks:

What scents or smells arouse you sexually?

Questions 12 and 13

These concern erotic arousal and drug use. Question 12 identifies the use of social drugs such as marijuana, hashish, cocaine, and amyl nitrite, and Question 13 asks what effects drugs have on the user during sexual activities. A checklist of possible effects can help the respondent to identify self-perception of drug effects. The Questions are phrased:

12. *What kind of mood-altering substances do you use to heighten erotic arousal?*

13. *What effect does the drug have on you sexually?*

> followed by

Does using _____ (drug):

pep you up?

make you come quicker?

heighten the sexual experience?

make the orgasm seem longer?

turn you off?

bring you down?

delay your orgasm?

Questions 14-21

Questions 14 through 21 provide possible clues to homosexuality but should not be considered definitive indicators of homosexual behavior or orientation.
    Question 14 asks about the respondent's sexual arousal while looking at his or her own nude body; the respondent is asked:

Are you sexually aroused by seeing yourself nude?

Question 15 is concerned with the respondent's sexual arousal as a result of visual stimuli during self-masturbation. This question is subtle but nevertheless important because it gives a hidden clue to homosexual behavior or interest. It is concerned with the visual stimulation of the total body and image as erotically arousing and, more specifically, with observance of the genitals as erotic stimuli in self-masturbation. This question is one of about a dozen clues to homosexual behavior in the inventory. Research indicates that homosexuals, especially male homosexuals, tend to look at their genitals when they masturbate more often than heterosexuals do. The two parts of Question 15, asked separately, are:

15. *(a) Do you look at your genitals when you masturbate?*

   (b) Are you aroused sexually by looking at yourself masturbating?

Questions 16 and 17 are concerned with the respondent's erotic arousal while seeing the opposite sex and the same sex nude. As is true of the first three questions in this block, the order and terminology used for these questions are dependent on the gender of the respondent. In taking a male history, the questions would be:

16. *Are you aroused sexually by seeing females in the nude?*

17. *Are you aroused sexually be seeing males in the nude?*

In taking a female history, the questions would be:

16. *Are you aroused sexually by seeing males in the nude?*

17. *Are you aroused sexually by seeing females in the nude?*

Questions 18 and 19 are concerned with the respondent's erotic arousal as a result of seeing specific body areas, culturally determined as erotic, of the respondent's own sex. For females, the body area is nude female breasts; for males, it is the naked erect penis. Obviously, which question is asked depends on the respondent's gender. In taking a female history, Question 19 is asked:

19. *Are you aroused sexually by seeing nude female breasts?*

In taking a male history, Question 18 is asked:

18. *Are you aroused sexually by seeing an erect, nude penis?*

Questions 20 and 21 ask about the respondent's erotic arousal to same-sex buttocks. These questions may be a clue to anal intercourse. A male respondent's affirmative response to questions about sexual arousal by seeing an erect penis or male buttocks may suggest a preference for fellation or anal intercourse.

Positive responses to these two questions from female respondents tend to indicate female homosexuality but provide no clue to preferred techniques. Most female homosexuals are not nearly so aroused by specific parts of the body as by the overall configuration of the body.

Once again, the questions asked are dependent on the gender of the respondent. In taking a female history, the question asked is:

21. *Are you aroused sexually by seeing nude female buttocks?*

Conversely, in taking a male history, the question is:

20. *Are you aroused sexually be seeing nude male buttocks?*

Questions 22-24

The next three questions (22, 23, and 24) provide possible clues to sadomasochistic (S/M) behavior. The sadist can be identified as the active participant, and the masochist as the passive participant.

Question 22 asks whether or not the respondent participates actively in any mildly sadistic behavior and whether he or she finds it erotically arousing. The question is asked in two parts:

22. *(a) When you are sexually excited, do you sometimes nibble, scratch, bite, pinch, or hit your partner?*

The respondent is first asked if he or she engages in the behavior, not whether or not the behavior causes arousal. If the answer is positive, then the interviewer asks:

22. *(b) Does this arouse you sexually?*

This division of the question is necessary because people often engage in behavior that is not particularly arousing for them merely to please their partners.

Question 23 concerns the respondent's erotic arousal as a passive participant in mild masochistic behavior:

23. *(a) During sex, are you sometimes bitten, nibbled, scratched, pinched, or hit?*

   (b) Does that arouse you?

Question 24 addresses the respondent's sexual arousal from reading about or seeing acts of torture, rape, bondage, violence, sadism, and masochism, etc. The phrasing of the question is designed to elicit whether or not the respondent is aroused by observing these acts, rather than to allow for a response concerning the subject's experience or participation (or lack of) in the activity. The question asked is:

Do reports or stories of violent behavior such as torture, rape, bondage cutting, and so forth, arouse you?

Question 25

Question 25 is concerned with the respondent's sexual arousal while watching animals copulate. The question is:

Are you aroused sexually by seeing animals have intercourse?

Examples of Responses and Coding

A. *Male, age 43, single (see Figure 23–3)*

1. *(a) Are you aroused sexually by thinking of females?*

   What do you mean by aroused?

   Well, I mean are you aware of any physiologic changes in your body? Is there warm skin, deep breathing, rapid pulse; do you get an erection or a semi-hard-on?

Oh yes, I understand what you mean. I am aroused by thinking of females.

1. *(b) Are you aroused sexually by thinking of males?*

   No, not very much, but occasionally.

2. *(a) Are you aroused sexually by seeing females in a social situation, like walking down the street or in a room?*

   Not really; it is a little exciting sometimes.

2. *(b) Are you aroused sexually by seeing males in a similar situation?*

   No, not at all.

3. *(a) Are you aroused sexually by seeing pictures of nude females?*

   Yes, that's arousing.

FIGURE 23-3. Male

3. *(b) How about pictures of nude males?*

Well, a little bit, not a great deal.

4. *Are you aroused sexually by seeing pictures of sexual acts where people are do-ing something?*

Oh, that gives me a terrific bang! I really enjoy that.

5. *Are you aroused sexually by seeing live shows?*

You mean like *Deep Throat?*

No, that's a movie. I mean live shows or theatrical productions, like Oh, Calcut-ta, Let My People Come, Hair. *Any show that is performed in front of an au-dience.*

Well, yeah! That turns me on quite a bit.

6. *Are you aroused sexually by seeing X-rated movies?*

Yes, I enjoy them very much.

7. *Are you aroused sexually by reading romantic love stories in books or maga-zines?*

Like what, for instance.

Romeo and Juliet, Love Story, *things like that.*

No, that doesn't do a thing for me.

8. *Are you aroused sexually by listening to music?*

Yes, I am.

What particular kinds of music or pieces do you find arousing?

Well, drums really turn me on, and I love lyrics and rock.

Any other kind?

No, that's really my biggest turn-on.

9. *Are you aroused sexually by motion; that is, by riding in an automobile or bus or train?*

I used to be when I was young, but no longer.

10. *Are you aroused sexually by alcohol?*

No, not really. It does lower my inhibitions and makes me freer, but it doesn't actually arouse me sexually.

11. *Are you aroused by any odors or smells?*

I love sweet perfume.

Anything else?

No.

12. *(a) You told me earlier in the history that you have used pot occasionally. How does it affect you sexually?*

Well, pot is a real turn-on for me. I think I can last longer with pot and get higher sexually with it.

How about LSD?

No, LSD doesn't do a thing for me sexually, it just gets me into my head.

What other mood-altering substances do you use?

Pot's my only bag.

12. *(c) Have you ever tried cocaine?*

No.

12. *(b) Hashish?*

No.

12. *(c) Amyl nitrite?*

No, nothing other than pot.

14. *Are you aroused sexually by seeing yourself nude in the mirror?*

No, that doesn't do anything for me.

15. *Do you sometimes look at your penis when you masturbate?*

Yes, I've done that sometimes, not often.

Okay.

16. *Are you aroused sexually by seeing females nude?*

Sure.

17. *Are you aroused sexually by seeing nude males?*

Yes, a bit, particularly if they have nice asses. I just love that. (Question 20 answered)

18. *Are you aroused sexually by seeing a nude erect penis?*

No, that doesn't do too much for me.

20. (Interviewer checking Question 20) *Are you aroused sexually by seeing male buttocks?*

You bet! I love a big-assed guy.

22. *When you have sex with a male or female, do you bite, nibble, scratch, hit, or pinch?*

Yeah, I do that a fair amount.

Does that turn you on?

Yes, I enjoy that.

23. *Are you sometimes pinched, nibbled, bitten, scratched, or hit during sex?*

Yes, that happens.

Does that arouse you?

Yes, but not as much as my doing it to my partner.

24. *Are you aroused by reading stories or hearing of incidents of violence, torture, rape, that kind of thing?*

No, that's a real turn-off for me.

25. *Are you aroused sexually by seeing two animals have intercourse together?*

No, I'm not into animals.

B. *Female, age 25, married, high school graduate (see Figure 23-4)*

1. *(a) Are you aroused sexually by thinking of males?*
Not very much.

1. *(b) Are you aroused sexually by thinking of females?*
No.

2. *(a) Are you aroused sexually by seeing males?*
Not at all.

2. *(b) Are you aroused sexually by seeing females.*
No.

3. *(a) Are you aroused sexually by seeing pictures of naked men?*
No, that disgusts me.

3. *(b) How about pictures of naked women?*
I don't like that either.

FIGURE 23-4. Female

4. (a) *Are you aroused sexually by seeing pictures of sex acts?*
   A little bit, if they are not dirty.

5. *Are you aroused sexually by seeing live sex shows?*
   I've never seen one.

6. *Are you aroused sexually by seeing X-rated movies?*
   They disgust me.

7. *Are you aroused sexually by reading romantic love stories?*
   Yes, that really turns me on.

8. *Are you aroused sexually by listening to music?*
   Yes. Rock and disco really lets me get it on.

9. *Are you aroused sexually by motion, that is by riding on a bus or train or a horse or bike?*
No.

10. *Are you aroused sexually by alcohol?*
It puts me to sleep.

11. *Are you aroused by an odor or smells?*
A little by men's aftershave.

12. *How does pot affect you sexually?*
It doesn't.

13. (Does not apply)

14. *Are you aroused sexually by seeing yourself naked?*
No.

15. (Does not apply because she does not masturbate)

16. *Are you aroused sexually by seeing naked men?*
No.

17. *Are you aroused sexually by seeing naked females?*
No.

18. *Are you aroused sexually by seeing an erect penis?*
No.

19. *Are you aroused sexually by seeing female breasts?*
No.

20. *Seeing male buttocks?*
No.

21. *Seeing female buttocks?*
No.

22. *Do you ever bite, nibble, scratch, or hit when you have sex?*
No.

23. *Are you bitten, nibbled, scratched, or hit when you have sex?*

Yes, sometimes.

24. *Does reading stories of rape or torture arouse you?*

No.

25. *Are you aroused by seeing two animals having intercourse?*

No, it disgusts me.

BACKGROUND INFORMATION

HEALTH			DREAMS		INCIDENTAL PROSTITUTION	
				PREMARITAL COITAL ATTITUDES		CONTRACEPTION
		PRE-ADOLESCENT SEX PLAY			EXTRA-MARITAL COITUS	
	EROTIC AROUSAL					
MARRIAGE						
			PREMARITAL PETTING	FIRST COITUS		INCIDENTAL HOMOSEXUALITY
		PUBERTY				
	FAMILY BACKGROUND				MARITAL COITUS	ANIMAL CONTACTS
ANATOMY		SELF-MASTURBATION	RECREATION	PREMARITAL COITUS		OTHER SEXUAL BEHAVIORS
	SEX EDUCATION		GROUP SEX			

FIGURE 24-1

24

Anatomy

The Anatomy block contains information on the physical structure and function of the respondent's body, body information, and physical features preferred in sexual partners. Much of the information asked is necessary to round out the person's sex history, but the interviewer may want to reorganize information in this block for special clinical or research use. For a person presenting, for example, vaginismus, transsexualism, or impotence, one might wish to explore questions of anatomy in considerably more detail. A series of checklists unique to this block have been provided to enable the interviewer to obtain detailed information.

Questions are organized so as to distinguish those that are asked of males only from those asked only of females. Questions 1 through 3 and 23 through 26 are asked of both females and males. Questions 4 through 15, however, are asked exclusively of male respondents, and Questions 16 through 22 exclusively of females.

The location of the Anatomy block in the recording sheet may be seen in Figure 24-1; the items that are explored are listed below, and responses are recorded as shown in Figure 24-2.

1. Height
2. Current weight
3. Maximum weight and age
4. Penis size flaccid
5. Penis size erect
6. Penis circumference flaccid
7. Penis circumference erect
8. Circumcision
9. Phimosis
10. Hypospadia
11. Number of descended testes
12. Preejaculatory fluid
13. Postejaculatory fluid
14. Direction of penis in erection
15. Curve of penis in erection
16. Female breast size
17. Female breast shape
18. Menstruation duration

19. Menstrual cycle
20. Menstrual regularity
21. Dysmenorrhea
22. Menstrual lubrication and arousability
23. Body-image changes
24. Body-image changes desired in sex partner
25. Perception of partner's feelings about respondent's body
26. Sex-partner preferences

FIGURE 24-2

Questions 1-3

Questions 1, 2, and 3, asked separately, are:

1. *How tall are you?*

2. *How much do you weigh?*

3. *What is the most you ever weighed in your life (not counting pregnancy) and how old were you when you weighed that much?*

Questions 4-15

These are concerned with aspects of the respondent's genital anatomy and are asked only of males.

4. *How long is your penis when it is soft?*

5. *How long is your penis in erection?*

6. *How many inches around your penis when it is soft?*

7. *How many inches around your penis when it is hard?*

8. *Are you circumcised?*

9. *Can you pull your foreskin over the head of your erect penis?*

10. *Is the opening of the penis out on the tip end or underneath?*

11. *Do you have two testes? Which hangs lower, the left or the right?*

The measurement of penis size contributes to anthropometric research and can either be estimated or actually calculated. Measurement of the erect penis is taken from the top of the penis against the body to the tip. Male respondents generally estimate the length of the penis in erection as shorter than it actually is because their downward visual angle distorts their perception and the pubic hair camouflages some of the length. Circumference of the penis is measured at the widest area of the shaft.

Question 8, on circumcision, is usually followed by the additional question, "Were you circumcised as a baby?" If the answer is negative, the interviewer elicits the respondent's age at the time of circumcision and records it as check (for yes) plus the age given. An **X** here means not circumcised.

If the respondent is circumcised, Question 9 is omitted since there can be no phimosis after circumcision. If the respondent has not been circumcised, Question 9 would be:

In erection, does the skin come over the head of your penis and, if it does, can you retract it?

In recording responses on phimosis, the interviewer can use the check system in the following manner:

X   no phimosis

✓   yes, phimosis*

+   the respondent wears the skin over the penis but the tip shows

−   the skin is all the way back but not as in circumcision

When asking Question 10 on hypospadia, it is very helpful for the respondent if the interviewer uses a thumb as a model for the penis, pointing to the tip of the thumb and underneath it to illustrate the opening at the tip of the penis or, in the case of hypospadia, the opening of the urethra underneath the penis.

Question 11 is presented in a telling fashion rather than an asking fashion: in other words, rather than "How many testes do you have?" the question is "Do you have two testes?" If the respondent has two testes, the interviewer asks, "Does one testis hang lower than the other?" and, if so, "Which one?" There are only three possible responses to this question: both testes hang at the same level, =, left testis hangs lower, L, or right testis hangs lower, R.

Questions 12 and 13 are concerned with ejaculatory fluid from the penis. Pre-ejaculatory fluid, often erroneously called precoital fluid, and postejaculatory fluid originate in the Cowpers glands and can be distinguished from semen in that it is thin, clear, and also delicately elastic in substance. It usually is emitted from the penis ten to fifteen minutes after ejaculation or from the urethra just before ejaculation. Younger men seem to experience pre- and postejaculatory fluid emission more frequently than do older men. Some men experience one and not the other; that is, they experience either preejaculatory mucous and not post-, or post- and not pre-. The significance of asking about pre- and postejaculatory fluid is that preejaculatory fluid may be an indicator of sexual arousal. At this point, the interviewer may want to do a little sex educating by informing the respondent of the possibility that sperm may be carried in preejaculatory fluid and contraception problems may result. The questions may be phrased as follows:

12. *Before you come, have you noticed a clear, slippery liquid that comes out the end of your penis?*

13. *After you come, do you notice the same clear, slippery liquid?*

Questions 14 and 15 help the interviewer identify the shape of the respondent's penis in erection. Question 14 is concerned with the angle of the penis at maximum erection:

14. *When the penis is hard, does it angle toward your legs or straight up against your belly or somewhere in between?*

*If the interviewer detects phimosis in a respondent, the following explanation of how to cure phimosis without surgery might be greatly appreciated. By inserting his fingers in the foreskin and pulling as hard as possible on it for about ten minutes twice a day for about two weeks, the respondent will be able to loosen the tight foreskin around the penis, making surgery unnecessary. This simple little trick to stretch the skin prevents unnecessary circumcisions in adult years.

The interviewer can clarify the question by diagramming many potential penile angles during erection or by using a pencil or a pen perpendicular to a table and moving the pencil a full 180 degrees in an up and down motion until the respondent can identify which angle most correctly reflects the direction of his penis during erection.

15. *(a) In erection, is your penis directly in front of you, or is it off to the left or the right, or up or down?*

The interviewer can again demonstrate by using a diagram or a pen or pencil. The second part of Question 15 is:

15. *(b) Does your penis curve up or down, left or right?*

Extreme curvature of the penis during erection can be the cause of some difficulty in intercourse and may be due to Peyronie's disease. Actual penis measurement may be done by the respondent in private and recorded in the history at a later time.

Questions 16-22

These are asked of females only and are concerned with the size and shape of breasts and with menstruation. The questions may be expanded to include, for example, clitoral and vaginal size, genital appearance, hymeneal strands, nipple size and color, and also to tap the respondent's feelings about specific body parts, their function, and the satisfaction or dissatisfaction the respondent feels about each. The comfort a respondent displays in answering questions about anatomy is an indication to the interviewer of how familiar the respondent is with her own body. The questions are:

16. *What size are your breasts?*

17. *Can you describe the shape of your breasts?*

18. *How many days do you flow?*

19. *How long a time is there between the beginning of one of your menstrual periods and the beginning of the next?*

20. *How regularly do you get your menstrual cycle?*

21. *Is there pain during menstruation, and if so, how long does it last?*

22. *Are there certain times of the month when you are more easily aroused sexually or have more vaginal lubrication than at other times? Such as just before menstruation, or during, or just after, or perhaps not close to menstruation at all?*

Questions 23-26

Questions 23 and 24 deal with body image and any changes the respondent would like for him or herself and for his or her sex partner's body:

23. *If you could change your body in any way, what would you change?*

24. *If you could change something about your sexual partner's body, what would it be?*

Question 25 asks:

How do you think your partner feels about your body?

Question 26 identifies specific body features that the respondent prefers in a sexual partner. The question is:

What particular characteristics do you prefer for your sex partner to have?

or

How do you like your sex partners to look?

The following checklist is useful in getting responses to questions 23, 24, and 26. The interviewer may want to ask all of the items for all three questions but record only those for which the response is positive.

masculine	feminine
hair (texture, curl, color)	complexion
body hair	muscle tone
arms	legs
thighs	buttocks
abdomen	hips
ears	nose
eyelids	face lift
breasts	nipples (size and color)
penis	scrotum
circumcised	vagina size
pubic hair	genitals

Examples and Coding of Responses

A. *Male, eighth-grade education, age 43 (see Figure 24-3)*

1. *How tall are you?*

   I'm 6 feet tall.

2. *How much do you weigh?*

   I weigh 160 lbs.

3. *What's the most you ever weighed in your life?*

   Uh, 200 lbs.

   How old were you then?

   I was in the Army.

Well, that made you about 20.

Yeah, that's right.

4. *When your penis is soft, how long would you guess it is?*

Oh, it ain't more than 4 inches.

5. *How long is your penis when it's hard?*

I don't know, I never measured it.

Well, make a guess. Would you say it's this long, this long, or this long? (Interviewer demonstrates possible length, with his or her hands, in no progression.)

About 6 inches.

8. *Have you ever been circumcised? Have you ever had skin cut away from the head of your penis?*

No, I guess I never did.

FIGURE 24-3. Male

6' 160 200	
6" 4" @20	
X X	
X ✓ L	
± X	
⊦ up	
5kn smth	
thnr	
≃	
Tall·rd hd·gd teeth	
smell gd - bg Br.	

9. *When your penis is hard, do you have any trouble pulling the skin back over the head?*

No, no trouble.

10. *Is the opening on your penis about here on the tip end or underneath?*

No, it's right there on the tip end.

11. *Do you have two balls?*

Uh, yeah.

Does one hang lower than the other?

Uh, I guess the left one does.

12. *Before you come, have you ever noticed any white—any clear, slippery liquid that hangs or comes off the end of your prick?*

Yeah, I noticed that sometimes.

13. *And how about a while after you come—have you ever noticed any of that same slippery fluid come out?*

No, I never did then.

14. *When your penis is hard, is it right straight in front of you or is it up right against your belly or somewhere in between?*

No, it sticks right out straight.

15. *Is it right straight in front of you or up to the left, or up or down?*

Well, it turns up a little bit.

23. *Would you want to change your body in any way at all? Is there any way you would change it?*

Oh, I guess I like my body pretty well.

Anything about your height or your weight or your hair or your skin?

Oh, I'd like smoother skin. I had acne when I was a kid.

Anything else about your body that you'd like to change?

No, I like it all right.

24. *Is there anything about your sex partner you'd like to change? Anything about her body?*

Well, she weighs about 30 pounds more than I'd like her to weigh, but outside of that, she's a pretty good-looking broad.

25. *How do you think your sex partner feels about your body?*
    She don't care.

26. *What kinds of things do you like in a sex partner?*
    I like 'em tall, redhead, good teeth, fun loving, and pretty smelling.

    Fine. Anything else?
    Yeah, big tits.

    O.K.

B. *Female, eighth-grade education, age 27 (see Figure 24–4)*

 1. *How tall are you?*
    I'm 5 feet 2.

 2. *And how much do you weigh?*
    I weigh 130 lbs.

FIGURE 24-4.   Female

3. *What's the most you ever weighed?*

Oh, this is the most I've ever weighed.

18. *How long are your menstrual periods?*

They're about four days.

19. *And how long is it from the beginning of one period to the beginning of the next?*

Oh, it comes about once a month.

Would you say it's every 28 days, or every 30 days?

Oh, I never kept track much, but I think about every 30 days.

20. *Do they come regular?*

Yeah, about as far as I can tell.

21. *Do you have any pain when you menstruate?*

Yeah, the first day, it's miserable.

22. *Have you noticed any times of the month when you are more easily aroused sexually than at other times? When there is more lubrication in your vagina? Is this before menstruation, or during, or after?*

I think it's right after I menstruate.

23. *If you could change your body in any way at all, is there anything you would like to change?*

Yeah, I'd like to lose 15 pounds. And my hair is stringy, I don't particularly like it, and I wish my nose was smaller. I thought of getting it fixed once upon a time but I didn't.

Anything about the rest of your body? How about your breasts?

No, I like my breasts. They're about right.

Anything about your complexion, about your shape, anything about your sex organs, anything you'd like to change?

No, I like myself pretty well.

24. *Anything about your sex partner that you'd change?*

I'd like him bigger. He's too skinny.

Anything else?

Not offhand—at least nothing I can't live with.

25. *How do you think your partner feels about your body?*

    Oh, he'd love me to be bigger.

26. *What preferences do you have for a sex partner?*

    I like someone who can perform, that's all.

    You mean sexually?

    Yeah, it don't matter too much about the rest of him.

    O.K.

BACKGROUND INFORMATION

HEALTH			DREAMS		INCIDENTAL
					PROSTITUTION
				PREMARITAL	CONTRACEPTION
		PRE-		COITAL	
		ADOLESCENT		ATTITUDES	EXTRA-
	EROTIC	SEX PLAY			MARITAL
	AROUSAL				COITUS
MARRIAGE					
			PREMARITAL	FIRST	INCIDENTAL
			PETTING	COITUS	HOMOSEXUALITY
		PUBERTY			
				MARITAL	ANIMAL
	FAMILY			COITUS	CONTACTS
	BACKGROUND				
ANATOMY				PREMARITAL	
		SELF-	RECREATION	COITUS	
		MASTURBATION			OTHER
					SEXUAL
					BEHAVIORS
	SEX				
	EDUCATION				
			GROUP SEX		

FIGURE 25-1

25

Group Sex

The information in the Group Sex block is very threatening and is usually asked near the end of the interview, but before Homosexuality and Animal Contacts.

Seeing one's parents having sex may be a joyful or traumatic experience or something in between. The interviewer may want to explore reactions to seeing and being seen and to record specific instances in abbreviated form below the block.

For elaborate group sex experiences, a more extensive questionnaire needs to be constructed, so that the dynamics and activities of group sex, including troilism (two men and one woman, or two women and one man), larger groups, swinging, etc., may be explored.

Figure 25–1 shows the Group Sex block's location on the recording sheet; Figure 25–2 shows the location of responses to the following questions:

1. Have you ever seen anyone having intercourse
2. Have you ever seen your parents having intercourse
3. (If the answer to Question 1 and/or Question 2 is yes) Were you sexually aroused by watching
4. Has anyone ever seen you having intercourse
5. Group sex:
   (a) Frequency
   (b) Number of people involved
   (c) Like or dislike it
   (d) Will you have more

Example of Responses and Coding

Female (see Figure 25–3)

1. *Have you ever seen anyone having intercourse?*

   Yes.

2. *Have you seen your parents having intercourse?*

   Yes. At 12 I barged into my parents' room while they were having intercourse. We were all embarrassed. I left at once.

3. *Were you sexually aroused when you watched them?*

   No.

4. *Has anyone ever seen you having intercourse?*

   Yes, my roommate on a double date.

5. *Have you ever had group sex?*

   Yes.

   (a) How often?

   Well, I think three times now.

FIGURE 25-2

	1 3	
	2	
	4	
	5	

FIGURE 25-3. Female

	✓ ✓	
	√acid @12 Xem	
	√dd	
	✓*	

*3x·w/♀ + 2♂ Like✓. Repeat nxt. wk.

(b) How many people were involved?

Myself, my girlfriend, her boyfriend, and his boyfriend.

Four of you?

Yes.

(c) Did you like it?

Definitely.

(d) Would you do it again?

Yes, in fact we have a date next week.

BACKGROUND INFORMATION						
HEALTH			DREAMS		INCIDENTAL PROSTITUTION	
				PREMARITAL COITAL ATTITUDES		CONTRACEPTION
		PRE-ADOLESCENT SEX PLAY			EXTRA-MARITAL COITUS	
	EROTIC AROUSAL					
MARRIAGE			PREMARITAL PETTING	FIRST COITUS		INCIDENTAL HOMOSEXUALITY
		PUBERTY				
	FAMILY BACKGROUND				MARITAL COITUS	ANIMAL CONTACTS
ANATOMY		SELF-MASTURBATION	RECREATION	PREMARITAL COITUS		OTHER SEXUAL BEHAVIORS
	SEX EDUCATION		GROUP SEX			

FIGURE 26-1

26

Incidental Homosexuality

Up to this point, the interview has tended to stress primarily heterosexual behavior. If the respondent has an extensive homosexual history, it is recorded on a separate inventory that has been developed to accommodate it (see Chapter 29). If the homosexual behavior has been only occasional or incidental, it is recorded in this block.

What is meant by "extensive" and "incidental" homosexuality? Generally, if a person has had more than four different partners *or* has had more than two or three years of homosexual behavior with moderate frequency *or* has a strong psychological homosexual component, the extensive homosexual inventory (Chapter 29) is used. An experienced interviewer will know when to use the long form. Also, by this time in the history the interviewer has some clues as to whether or not there is a homosexual history from responses to questions on fantasy and masturbation, sexual arousal, and the like. An interviewer never asks, "Have you had homosexual relations or experience?" The activity, like all sexual activities, is assumed.

The position of the Incidental Homosexuality block is indicated in Figure 26-1. The information sought in this block is listed below. Figure 26-2 shows where it is recorded.

1. Age or ages involved
2. First experience
3. Frequency
4. Techniques used
5. Approached
6. Where
7. Attitude toward male homosexuality
8. Attitude toward female homosexuality
9. Homosexual friends
10. Choose spouse
11. Any more in future

FIGURE 26-2

	1
	2
	3
	4
	5 6
	7 8
	9
	10
	11

Question 1

Question 1 is concerned with the respondent's postpubescent homosexual experience.

After _____ (age at puberty), how young were you the first time you ever had a homosexual experience?

    or

After _____ (age at puberty), how young were you the first time you ever had sexual relations with someone of the same sex?

Question 2

This is an exploration of the respondent's first homosexual experience, including such factors as the circumstances in which it occurred, the age of the partner, its effects on the respondent and his or her feelings about it, and techniques. The questions, asked separately, are:

How did your first homosexual experience occur?

How old was your partner?

What techniques were used?

How did you feel about the experience?

Question 3

Question 3 asks about the frequency of incidental homosexual experience. As in other blocks, identifying frequencies of activity requires a series of questions. For instance, the peg system may be used to isolate blocks of time in the respondent's life. Such questions might be phrased:

How frequently since that first experience have you had homosexual experience?

When was the last homosexual experience you've had?

Between ages _____ and _____, how frequently . . . ?

When you lived in _____, how frequently . . . ?

What other homosexual experiences have you had?

Question 4

What techniques have been used in the sexual activity? (Masturbation—active, passive, or mutual; oral sex; or anal intercourse are the most common techniques.)

Questions 5 and 6

These are concerned with whether or not the respondent has been approached by any other (or any) homosexuals seeking contact and, if so, where these approaches took place. Even those respondents who report no first experience are asked the remaining questions in the block. Approaches typically take place through friends, in bars, on the street, at movies, discos, baths, gyms, gay establishments, etc., and the interviewer may want to administer a checklist to the respondent. The questions asked are:

5. *Have you had other homosexual approaches?*

    or

    Have you ever been approached by a homosexual or a person seeking homosexual contact?

6. *Where were the approaches made?*

Questions 7 and 8

Questions 7 and 8 are concerned with the respondent's attitudes about other people who have homosexual relations. The questions asked are:

7. *What do you think about two males having homosexual relations? Do you approve? Are you neutral? Do you disapprove?*

The same set of questions is asked for females and recorded separately in space 8.

CODING EXAMPLES

Responses to Questions 7 and 8 can best be recorded by using the symbols $>$, meaning greater than, and $<$, meaning less than, as illustrated in the following examples. A check, ν, is used to note approval, an **X** for disapproval, and an equal sign, $=$, for a neutral attitude.

	Response Examples	*Recordings*
(a)	I like women together sexually better than men.	♀ $>$ ♂
(b)	I disapprove of females, but I don't have any feelings about men together for sexual purposes.	**D** ♀ **N** ♂
(c)	Neither of the sexes should be having sexual relations with each other!	**D** ♂ + ♀
(d)	I approve of both men and women in homosexual behavior.	**A** ♂ + ♀
(e)	It doesn't make any difference to me.	**N** ♂ + ♀
(f)	Homosexuals will die in hell.	**D** ν ν ♂ + ♀
(g)	If it's all right for the people doing it, it's okay with me.	**A** ♂ + ♀

Question 9

Question 9 concerns the respondent's feelings about homosexual friends.

Suppose you learned that a good friend was homosexual. Would that affect your friendship?

In what ways?

Question 10

This constitutes yet another inquiry into the respondent's attitudes toward homosexuality. The information sought reflects the respondent's feelings about the same-sex partners in a deeper, more intimate sense. To get at such submerged attitudes, the information is couched in a question which asks the respondent to make a choice between a heterosexual and a homosexual experience for a spouse or current sex partner:

If you had to choose someone for your spouse (or current sex partner) to have sex with, would you choose someone of the same sex or the opposite sex?

Question 11

Question 11 is concerned with whether the respondent expects to have any or any more homosexual experiences in the future:

Do you think you will ever have homosexual relations in the future?

or

Will you have more homosexual relations?

Examples of Responses and Coding

A. *Male, age 35, never married (see Figure 26–3)*

1. *How young were you the first time you had a homosexual experience?*

   I was 15.

2. *Tell me, how did your first experience occur?*

   I was in boarding school, and my roommate came over one night and came to bed with me, and started to masturbate me.

   How did you feel about that?

   I was a little frightened, but not too upset.

   Did you masturbate him?

   No, I didn't.

   Did you do anything else?

   No.

   Recorded as: **Brd, rm, apprch, M$_p$ frite ± OK** (boarding school, roommate, approached; masturbation passive, fright, but experience was OK).

FIGURE 26-3.   Male

	15-16 +20
	Brd, rm approch Mp frite ±OK
	15-16 4xMp 20=2x cd rm GOm
	GOm
	✓ Bar, Frnd
	No♂<♀
	-Kp
	♂>♀
	X ?

3. *How frequently in boarding school was there homosexual activity?*

   That only occurred four times at 15 and 16.

   What other homosexual experiences have you had?

   Twice in college, I was a junior; again a roommate approached me and we had mutual fellation.

Any other experiences?

That's been the extent of it.

4. *What techniques have been used?*

Only mutual fellation.

Was there any intercourse?

No, just oral-genital stimulation.

O.K.

5. *Have you had other homosexual approaches?*

Yes, I've had several.

6. *Where did they occur?*

They occurred in a bar; they occurred on the street; and a married friend of mine approached me at his place.

Fine.

7. *How do you feel about two males who have sex with each other?*

It's their business, not mine.

Would you say you approve, you're neutral, or you disapprove?

I'd say I'm neutral.

8. *How do you feel about two females who have sex with each other?*

I guess I'm more approving of that than two males.

9. *Suppose you had a good friend who you learned was homosexual. Would your relationship with him be affected?*

What do you mean?

Would his homosexuality affect your friendship for him?

Well, I'm not sure. . . . I think I would keep him as a friend, but I don't think that we'd be quite as close to each other.

O.K.

10. *If you had a wife, and you had to choose another man or woman for her to have sex with, which sex would you choose for her?*

Oh, a man.

Why?

Well, I just don't know, but it seems more natural.

11. *Do you think you'll have more homosexual relations in the future?*

I don't think so, but I'm not sure because the experiences I've had weren't planned.

O.K.

FIGURE 26-4.   Female

	15 + 20
	frnd 15 Mm
	2 = 3x
	Mm X GO
	1x col rm
	D♂ A♀
	Kp
	♀
	-?

B. *Female, age 26, never married (see Figure 26-4)*

1. *After you started menstruating, at the age of 12, when was the first time you ever had sex with another female?*

   I had a girlfriend in high school and I was a sophomore and I was about 15 when that happened.

   All right, and how old was she?

   She was the same age.

2. *Tell me what happened.*

   Oh, she came over to spend the night and we were sleeping in bed and she put her arms around me and we started to hug and kiss and I got all worked up and reached over and felt her sex organs and she felt mine and we began to play with each other and we both came.

   How did you enjoy the experience?

   Well, it was sort of strange and it felt funny, but it sure felt good.

3. *Okay, after that, how frequently did you have sex with her?*

   Oh, we just got together one other time that year and then we just felt too funny about it and stopped.

5. *Okay, when was the next time you had sex with a female?*

   Well, I had that just one more time when I was in college, and my roommate and I did about the same thing.

   (Subject answers Question 6.)

   That means you've only had it with two girls three times—a total of three times?

   Yes, that's right.

4. *And the technique used was mutual masturbation?*

   Yes.

   Did you have any oral sex?

   No, there wasn't any oral sex. That's all there was.

8. *And how do you feel about two other women who have sex with each other?*

   Well, it's all right with me if it's all right with them.

7. *How do you feel about two men who have sex with each other?*

   Well, I don't approve of that quite as much because I think that they can go out and find somebody if they want to.

9. *Suppose you had a good friend, a female friend, and learned she was homosexual. Would that affect your friendship with her?*

No, I don't think it would.

10. *Suppose you had to choose for your boyfriend to have sex with a male or a female. Which would you choose for him?*

Oh, a female, of course.

11. *Do you think you'll ever have any more sex with females in the future?*

I really don't know—it's possible but I don't plan on it.

BACKGROUND INFORMATION						
HEALTH			DREAMS		INCIDENTAL	
					PROSTITUTION	
				PREMARITAL		CONTRACEPTION
		PRE-		COITAL		
		ADOLESCENT		ATTITUDES	EXTRA-	
	EROTIC	SEX PLAY			MARITAL	
	AROUSAL				COITUS	
MARRIAGE						
			PREMARITAL	FIRST		INCIDENTAL
			PETTING	COITUS		HOMOSEXUALITY
		PUBERTY				
					MARITAL	ANIMAL
	FAMILY				COITUS	CONTACTS
	BACKGROUND					
ANATOMY				PREMARITAL		
		SELF-	RECREATION	COITUS		
		MASTURBATION				OTHER
						SEXUAL
						BEHAVIORS
	SEX					
	EDUCATION					
			GROUP SEX			

FIGURE 27-1

27
Animal Contacts

Zoophilia or bestiality is deriving gratification from having sexual relations with animals. This is a threatening and taboo subject for many people, and this block is therefore usually presented at the end of the interview. If, however, there are premonitory signs revealed earlier in the history, these questions may be asked at that time. Areas where the interview may reveal clues to animal contacts are in the Masturbation, Dreams, and Erotic Arousal blocks. Responses in these blocks could be natural leads to the questions on Animal Contacts.

If the subject is one who experiments with sexual behavior, lives in a rural area, or gives any clues that he or she has had animal contacts, then the first question is "When was the first time you had sex with an animal?" If there are no clues that would indicate Animal Contacts, then the interviewer asks, "Have you ever had sex with an animal?"

Male contact with animals usually takes the form of vaginal intercourse with the animal. The most common female sexual behavior with animals is genital-oral contact, where the female is passive and the animal active. In addition, females are more likely to report body contact with animals and males are more likely to report having masturbated animals.

Figure 27–1 indicates the position of the Animal Contacts block. The items covered are indicated below. Figure 27–2 shows the location of responses.

1. Ages when animal contacts occurred
2. Frequency of contacts with each animal
3. Different animals involved
4. Techniques used with each

Examples of Recording and Coding

A. *Female, age 68, a widow for the past 28 years, and very shy (see Figure 27-3)*

1. *You've indicated that you are sometimes sexually aroused by seeing animals having intercourse in the street and that you often have fantasies about sexual contact with dogs. When was the first time you had sex with an animal?*

    (Long pause) I don't think I'd like to talk about it.

    This is painful and upsetting to you.

    Yes, it is.

FIGURE 27-2

	1
	2
	3
	4

FIGURE 27-3. Female

	58-66
	1
	Dog
	GOp

You somehow feel this is wrong.

No, I really don't feel it's wrong, but I know what society would think if they knew about this.

You should realize that this interview is completely confidential, always taken in code, and that nobody will know about it.

Yes, I guess it is a relief just to be able to talk about it.

When was the first time you had sex with an animal?

Well, I did with my dog Tony about ten years ago.

All right, you were about 58 then.

I had a little Yorkshire and he was the only "person" I had to love and he was very dear to my heart.

O.K., tell me how it began.

He was snuggling against me in bed and he began to lick me down there. It felt very good, and then better and better until suddenly I exploded in orgasm.

(Techniques used was answered here. There is no need to ask Question 4.)

2. *How often were you having sex with your dog ten years ago?*

I would say about once a week.

And is the dog still with you now?

No, he died two years ago.

And have you gotten another dog?

No, I couldn't bring myself to get another dog.

So for about eight years, you were having sex with your dog.

Yes, that's right.

You say you were averaging about once a week?

Yes, that's about right.

How do you feel about this?

I don't feel any way about it. People do many different things in their lives, and this is one of them. I wasn't harming anybody, and I don't think that it is anyone's particular business one way or the other.

Great.

3. *What other animals have you had sex with?*

No other ones, just my little dog.

Thank you.

B. *Male, age 18, high school graduate, unmarried, lives on a ranch (see Figure 27–4)*

1. *When was the first time you had sex with an animal?*

I was fourteen. I was alone in the south pasture with my prize heifer.

All right.

FIGURE 27-4.   Male

	14–16
	8x(-15)12@16
	Heifer·Dog·More try
	c

2. *How often were you having sex with your heifer?*

Well, I guess about eight times.

O.K.

3. *What other animals have you had sex with?*

There was my collie, too. And I did try the mare once, but it didn't work out because she has a temper and I was scared that she might kick me.

2. *How often were you having sex with your collie?*

Oh, about once a month the year I was 16.

What other sexual contacts with animals have you had?

That's all.

4. *What techniques did you use?*

With the heifer I talked quietly with her—she was small so I just stood there and put it in her.

O.K., what about the collie?

Oh, my collie. I was on my knees and I put it in her. She was real quiet and seemed to really like it. But the mare, well, I tried to stand on the fence and put it in, but she was restless and I was scared. She has a temper, so I gave up and left her alone.

BACKGROUND INFORMATION						
HEALTH			DREAMS		INCIDENTAL	
					PROSTITUTION	
				PREMARITAL		CONTRACEPTION
		PRE-		COITAL		
		ADOLESCENT		ATTITUDES	EXTRA-	
	EROTIC	SEX PLAY			MARITAL	
	AROUSAL				COITUS	
MARRIAGE						
			PREMARITAL	FIRST		INCIDENTAL
			PETTING	COITUS		HOMOSEXUALITY
		PUBERTY				
					MARITAL	ANIMAL
	FAMILY				COITUS	CONTACTS
	BACKGROUND					
ANATOMY				PREMARITAL		
		SELF-	RECREATION	COITUS		
		MASTURBATION				OTHER
						SEXUAL
						BEHAVIORS
	SEX					
	EDUCATION					
			GROUP SEX			

FIGURE 28-1

28

Other Sexual Behaviors

This block is a checklist or a "finding list" of other sexual behaviors. Its position is indicated in Figure 28-1. If a response is positive for any of the following items, an expanded series of questions will be needed. With the exception of transsexualism, the following behaviors are rarely found in females.

1. FETISHES

What fetishes do you have?

or

Are there any articles of clothing such as high heels, panties, leather goods, etc., that turn you on sexually?

2. TRANSVESTISM

(Male) *Have you ever worn articles of women's clothing?*

and

Did this arouse you sexually?

(Female) *Have you ever worn men's clothing?*

and

Did this arouse you sexually?

3. TRANSSEXUALISM (Male and Female)

Have you ever wanted to be the opposite gender (sex)?

Have you ever felt you were the opposite gender (sex)?

Have you ever considered surgery for changing your sex?

4. EXHIBITIONISM

(Male) *Have you ever deliberately exposed your penis in a public place?*

(Female) *Have you ever exposed your breasts and/or genitals in a public place?*

5. VOYEURISM (Peeping)

Have you ever done any peeping?

6. PEDOPHILIA

Have you ever wanted to have sex with a pubescent or preadolescent person?

Have you ever had sex with a pubescent or preadolscent person?

7. RAPE OR SEXUAL ASSAULT

(Male) *Have you ever forced a person to have sex with you?*

(Female) *Have you ever been forced into having sex?*

I	II	III	IV	V	VI	
	CONTACTS AND AGES					
			PARTNER PREFERENCE		PROSTITUTION	
FIRST EXPERIENCE		PETTING TECHNIQUES				
				SOCIAL CONFLICTS		
					SELF-ANALYSIS	
	SOCIAL POSITION					
		PARTNER ORGASM		HOMOSEXUAL INDICATORS		
			SOURCES OF CONTACTS			
		SUBJECT ORGASM				
	RELATIONSHIPS					
	RACIAL BACKGROUND					
		DEMOGRAPHICS OF ORGASM				

FIGURE 29-1

29

Homosexual Inventory

A separate inventory and coding form have been developed for people who have extensive homosexual histories. These persons may also have a different life style, a different way of looking at their environment, and a different vocabulary from the rest of the population. An entirely new set of questions was developed to identify and to accommodate some of these differences.

The homosexual inventory form is shown in Figure 29-1. The block areas are organized into groups of questions that explore first experience, techniques, and frequency (Column I); characteristics of the partners—occupations, racial groups, etc. (Column II); petting techniques used and frequency of orgasm (Column III); partner preferences and sources of contacts (Column IV); special difficulties as a result of homosexual behavior, and subliminal or overt indicators of homosexual orientation (Column V); and homosexual prostitution and self-perception (Column VI). Although the questions in this inventory represent a detailed overview of homosexual behavior, a more extensive exploration of a given area of behavior, attitudes, or adjustment may be developed to suit the research, clinical, or educational needs of the professionals who will be using the inventory.

COLUMN I: FIRST EXPERIENCE

The questions asked in the First Experience block are listed below. Responses are coded on the lines indicated in Figure 29-2.

FIGURE 29-2

I	II	III	IV	V	VI	
1	1	1	1	1	1 2	
2 a b	2	2a	2	2	3	
3	3	b c	3	3	4	
4	4	d	4	4	5	
5	5	e	5	5	6	
6	6	3	6	6	7	
7	7	4	7	7	8	
8	8	5	8 9	8 a	1a b	
9	1	6	10	b	2	
10	2	7	11	c	3	
11	3	8	12	d	4	
12	4	9	13	9a b	5	
13	5	10	14	10a b	6	
14	6	11	15	11	7	
15	7	12	1	12	8	
	8	13	2		9	
	9	14	3	Sub Interv.		
	10	15	4	1		
	11	1	5	2		
	12	2	6	3		
	13	3 4	7 8	4		
	14	5	9	5		
	15	6	10	6		
	16	7	11	7		
	17	1	12	8		
	18	2	13	9		
	19	3	14	10		
	1	4	15	11		
	2	5	16	12		
	3	6	17			
	4	7	18			
	5	8	19			
	6		20 21			
	1	1	22			
	2	2	23			
	3	3	24			
	4	4	25			
	5	5	26			
	6	6	27			
			28			
			29			

1. Age
2. (a) Partner's age
   (b) Relation of partner to respondent
3. Circumstances
4. Sexual techniques
5. Satisfaction

Questions concerning the respondent's first experience with homosexual behavior include the respondent's age at the time of the first experience, the partner's age and relation to the respondent, the circumstances in which the experience took place, including the place of contact, the financial arrangements, and who made the initial approach, the sexual techniques employed, including passive, active, or mutual involvement, and the satisfaction of the experience for the respondent. The questions are phrased and asked in the following sequences:

1. *After puberty, how young were you the first time you had a homosexual experience?*

2. *(a) What age was your partner at the time?*

   (b) What relation was your partner to you?

         or

   How did you meet your partner?

3. *What were the circumstances which led to your first experience?*

   Where was the contact made?

   Who initiated the approach?

   What were the financial arrangements?

         or

   Was there any payment?

4. *What sexual techniques were used on the first experience?*

   Did you do that to you partner or did you partner do it to you, or did you do it to each other?

   The interviewer may use the following techniques as a checklist: masturbation, oral sex, anal intercourse, between the legs sex, and body contact.

5. *How much did you enjoy your first experience?*

Techniques: Age of First Experience

Questions 6 through 11 concern the respondent's age at the first experience of different technqies. They differ slightly for males and females and in both cases are asked twice in order to distinguish between the behavior done to the respondent by his or her partner (passive participation), and the behavior that the respondent did to the partner, (active participation). These six lines of the column are divided by a vertical line; responses on the left side of the line indicate passive participation; those on the right concern active participation. It is important to record the information on both side of the column for every respondent to determine the extend of the initial involvement in homosexual behavior.

The only difference between the male and the female histories is the techniques used. The items are as follows:

MALE HISTORY

Passive Participation (behavior done to the respondant)	*Active Participation* (respondent does the behavior to partner)
6. Manual masturbation	6. Manual masturbation
7. Fellatio	7. Fellatio
8. Anal coitus	8. Anal coitus
9. Interfemoral coitus	9. Interfemoral coitus
10. Full body contact	10. Full body contact
11. Anal fist stimulation (penetration)	11. Anal fist stimulation (penetration)

FEMALE HISTORY

Passive Participation	*Active Participation*
6. Manual masturbation	6. Manual masturbation
7. Cunnilingus	7. Cunnilingus
8. Anal stimulations (insertions)	8. Anal stimulation (insertions)
9. Breast stimulation to orgasm	9. Breast stimulation to orgasm
10. Tribadism	10. Tribadism
11. Vaginal stimulation (insertions)	11. Vaginal stimulation (insertions)

Interfemoral coitus is coming to orgasm by placing the penis between a man's legs; in lower social level vernacular this is called "leggins." Tribadism, also known as "bull dyking," involves body contact between two females. The questions asked of a male respondent's passive participation are as follows:

How young were you the first time—

6. *you were masturbated by another male?*

7. *another male put his mouth on your penis?*

8. *another male put his penis in your anus?*

9. *another male put his penis between your legs?*

10. *another male ever came by body contact alone with you?*

11. *another male manually penetrated your anus?*

To elicit information on the male respondent's active participation, the phrasing is changed to:

How young were you the first time—

6. *you ever brought another male to climax by masturbating him?*

7. *you put your mouth on another male's penis?*

8. *you put your penis in another male's anus?*

9. *you put your penis between another male's legs?*

10. *you came by full body contact alone?*

11. *you manually penetrated another male's anus?*

A female respondent is asked the following questions regarding her passive experiences of the different techniques:

How young were you the first time—

6. *another female brought you to orgasm by manually stimulating your genitals?*

7. *another female put her mouth on your genitals?*

8. *another female brought you to orgasm by using a dildo for anal intercourse with you?*

9. *another female brought you to orgasm by stimulating your breasts?*

10. *another female brought you to orgasm through dry fucking?*

11. *another female brought you to orgasm by using a dildo for vaginal intercourse with you?*

Concerning female active participation, the questions are:

How young were you the first time you brought another female to orgasm by—

6. *stimulating her genitals with your fingers?*

7. *putting your mouth on her genitals?*

8. *using a dildo on her for anal intercourse?*

9. *stimulating her breasts?*

10. *dry fucking?*

11. *by using a dildo for vaginal intercourse?*

Frequencies

Questions 12 through 15 are concerned with the frequencies of homosexual contacts. The four questions (shown recorded in Figure 29–2) are:

12. Frequency first year   14. Maximum in one day
13. Maximum in one week   15. Average per week per year

Question 12 elicits the frequency of homosexual contacts during the first year, which is identified separately from frequencies during later years because frequency of first-year contacts often tend to be critical indicators of how rapidly an individual becomes fully involved in homosexual behavior. Question 13 asks the maximum frequency of homosexual contacts in any consecutive seven-day period; Question 14 the maximum frequency of homosexual contacts in any single day (defined as any twenty-four-hour period and singled out because many people report high rates of activity in a given day); and Question 15 asks the frequencies throughout the rest of the homosexual history, as measured in averages per week. The questions may be asked as follows:

12. *How frequently did you have homosexual contacts during the first year?*

    or

    When you were _____ years old, how frequently did you have homosexual contacts?

Examples of Responses and Coding

A. *Female, age 35, never married, two years of college (all coded responses for this subject throughout the chapter are shown in Figure 29–3)*

 1. *How old were you the first time you had a homosexual experience?*

    I was 14.

 2. *And how old was your partner?*

    My partner was a girlfriend of mine who was also 14.

 3. *What was the situation—how did you happen to have that first homosexual experience?*

    She came home and spent the night with me, and we got to fooling around, and we talked with each other to a degree, and I began to feel very much aroused, and I had an orgasm.

    Did she have an orgasm too?

    No, I don't think so.

 4. *Was there touching of genitalia?*

    No, it was just pretending to have intercourse on top of each other.

FIGURE 29-3. Female, age 35

35						♀	
14		15	1		♀	X	X X
14	frnd	67%	X		=	X	X
5 4.		2/15	(		±	X	X
BD	xcli	45 (29)			=	X	X
✓		3/15			X	X	X
19	19	14 (14)	✓	✓	0	fI nwX	X
21	23	own	✓	✓	0	✓	—
X	X	intrst	✓	✓	0	X	5 5
X	19	X	✓	✓	=	X	X
19	19	X	✓	✓		0	✓ chld
X	28	5	✓	✓	✓	0	✓
1/2		X	✓	✓	♀ mat	X x	X
10/		X	0	0	♀	X X	X
2/d		X	0	0	cult humn.	±	
X (-18)		2	X	X	12	75	up to her
1/(-21)		X	X	X	3		?
1/4 (-24)		X	X	X	X		
7/(-28)		1	X	X		X	X
2/(-d)		1	100				X
		X	5				X
		X	90	0			—
		1	X		3		X
		100	0		X		X
		X	5				—
		4	100				X
		1	X				X
		2	5				X
		3y	90				X
		1	X				X
		m	0				
		3	5				
		X	X				
		0					
		X	X				
		1=Phil	—				
		X	✓				
		X	—				
		X	✓				
		X	Hm. othr				

5. *Did you enjoy the situation?*

Yes, I did, very much.

6. *How old were you the first time you climaxed by being masturbated by a female?*

Oh, that wasn't until college—I must have been 19.

7. *And how old were you the first time you ever came by a woman putting her mouth on your genitalia?*

That was a little later. I must have been around 21.

8. *When did you first have your anus stimulated by another woman?*

I never did.

9. *When did you first come to climax by breast stimulation alone?*

That's never occurred for me.

6. *O.K. When was the first time you ever brought another female to climax by masturbating her?*

Oh, that was in college, and I was about 19.

7. *When was the first time you ever went down on a female and brought her to climax?*

That was about 23.

8. *When did you ever stimulate the anus of another woman?*

I never did.

9. *And have you ever brought a female to climax by stimulating her breasts?*

Yes, there was one girl only, I remember, in college. I was about 19 when that happened.

10. *And when did you first bring a female to climax by tribadism with her?*

That was also at 19.

Did you come then too?

Yes.

11. *When did you first have homosexual relations by having something inserted in your vagina?*

Never.

And when did you first insert something in another woman's vagina?

That happened once when I was 28.

12. *O.K. Back at 14, that first year that you were having homosexual relations, how often did you have them in that year?*

Well, with this one girl, we'd get together maybe once every two weeks in that year.

13. *What would be the maximum number of times in any week that you've ever had sex with a female?*

Oh, that woman I was living with—maybe ten times.

14. *And how about the most number of times in a day?*

Probably twice.

15. *All right—the rest of high school, say ages 15 to 17, how frequent was it?*

No, it stopped completely. There was none then.

And in college, how frequent was it?

Well, then it started up again, and I'd say it was once a week, through college.

And from 22 to 25, how frequently?

Well, then it went downhill again. It was about once a month.

And from 25 to 30?

Well, from 25 to 28, I was living with a woman, and we had sex practically every day, seven times a week.

And from 29 to 35?

Oh, now it's been, I'd say twice a week would be a fair average.

B. Male, age 30, never married, tenth-grade education (all coded responses for this subject throughout the chapter are shown in Figure 29-4)

1. *How old were you the first time you ever came with another male?*

Well, that was the first time I ever came. I must have been about 12.

2. *And how old was the other male?*

Oh, he was older. He was 18.

3, 4. *And what was the situation? How did you happen to have contact with him?*

I went down to the park and I knew some of my friends were going down there, and I met a guy in the toilet in the park, and he blew me.

FIGURE 29-4. Male, age 30

30							♂
12		1,000	5		♂	X	X X
18 strng		25%	20x		✓	±	f± $10-20
Trm prk		75%	21-d 10		= x fat	o	—
GOp xpay		72(29)	Bth		=	X	X
✓		X			✓	✓ lost job	X
12	9	15(12)	✓	✓	✓✓	X	—
12	12	45-50	✓	✓	✓	X	X
15	X	care for me-settled	✓	✓	✓ clean	✓	4-5 5
X	16	✳	✓	✓	o	IX 1x=$100	X
X	17		✓	✓	rough	X	✓
X	X		✓	✓	=	1 nite	✓
1/4			✓	✓	♂	X 1x=$100	X
25/			✓	✓	=	X 2-3x	✓
5/d			✓	✓	assrt. strng	✓	X
1/(-16)			✓	✓	10	50%	✓
5/(-22)			✓	✓	90		easy fun —
6/(-d)			X	X	✓		wht. f.
			1x·urin X		X	X X	
			80		—		X	
			—		✓		X	
			✓ ±		✓		X	
			X		✓		X	
		90%	X		✓		X	
		10%			f✓		X	
		(PS)	100		—		X	
		20%	2-3x		—		X	
		X	—		X		X	
		19	80				X	
		90%	X				X	
		P	20				
		2	X	X			
		0	X	X			
		0					
		X	X				
		5	X	✓			
		—	✓	X			
		X	=				
		X	✓				
			Nm. othr. Trm.				
			bch. bth				

Did he pay for you it?

No, no payment.

5. *Did you enjoy the experience?*

Yeah, it was exciting.

6. *And the first time you ever came by being jacked off by a male?*

Probably 12, too.

And the first time you ever made another male come by masturbating him?

Well, that was way back when I was 9 years old.

7. *When was the first time you ever made another male come by blowing him?*

Probably that same year—when I was 12.

8. *When was the first time you ever came by fucking another male?*

Oh, that wasn't until I was 15.

And when was the first time another male ever came in you?

Well, that's never happened. I don't like that—it hurts.

9. *Have you ever come just by putting your penis between a male's legs?*

Oh, I can't ever remember that happening.

Has another male ever come that way with you?

Oh, yeah, when I was 16, I guess that happened a bit.

10. *Have you ever come just by full body contact with a male?*

No, but a friend of mine came that way with me once when I was 17.

11. *Have you ever done fist fucking?*

No.

Or been fist fucked?

No.

12. *O.K. Back at 12—that first year—how often were you having homosexual contacts?*

Well, then it was just like going down to the park, and that was maybe a dozen times that year.

13. *What's the most number of times that you've ever had sex in a single week?*

14, 15. Well, when I've cruised tearooms, it's been as much as five times a day. Probably in a week, it would be 25 times.

15. *All right, until you quit school, from 13 to 16, how frequently were you having homosexual relations?*

Probably once a week.

And from 17 to, say, 22, how often was it?

Oh, five times a week probably.

And from 22 to now?

It's nearly every night—I'd say six times a week.

COLUMN II: PARTNERS

The second column of the Homosexual Inventory has four subsections that are concerned with the number of homosexual contacts the respondent has had, the ages of the partners, their social positions, the respondent's relationships with them, and their racial groupings.

Contacts and Ages

Information on the total number of partners and their ages is grouped in the first block of the column. The eight questions in this block are as follows:

1. Total number of contacts
2. Percent same age as subject
3. Percent older than subject
4. Age of oldest partner and respondent's age at occurrence
5. Percent younger than subject
6. Age of youngest partner and respondent's age at occurrence
7. Age preference
8. Why

As in the heterosexual inventory, getting at the total number of contacts (Question 1) may require several questions, and unless the respondent has maintained a detailed record of his or her contacts, the best information will be an approximation or estimate of the total count.

Question 2 is concerned with the number of partners or the percentage of partners (if that's the only way the information can be estimated) who were approximately the same age as the respondent. The estimation generally includes a five-year range on either side of the subject's age.

Question 3 concerns the percentage of homosexual contacts who were significantly older than the subject; again, older is defined as five or more years older.

Question 4 asks the age of the oldest person with whom the respondent has ever had homosexual contact, and the age of the respondent when this contact occurred.

Question 5 asks for the number or percentage of homosexual contacts who are significantly (also defined as five or more years) younger than the subject. (The interviewer can check the respondent's accuracy in identifying partners by their ages by adding the numbers given in response to Questions 2, 3, and 5; the total should equal 100 percent.)

Question 6 asks the age of the youngest person with whom the respondent has ever had a homosexual contact and the respondent's age at the time of this contact.

Question 7 asks the age or age range of the partners the respondent prefers, and Question 8 asks the respondent to explain this preference.

The questions asked are:

1. *What is the total number of homosexual partners you've had?*

2. *How many of these partners would you say are approximately your own age?*

3. *How many would you say are older than you?*

4. *What is the age of the oldest partner you've ever had?*

   How old were you then?

5. *How many of your partners would you say are younger than you?*

6. *What is the age of the youngest homosexual partner you've ever had?*

   How old were you then?

7. *What age partners do you prefer?*

8. *Why?*

Examples of Responses and Coding

A. *Female, age 35*

1. *How many different homosexual partners have you had?*

   Well, I guess I could almost count them. There was a girl in high school, and there were three in college, that's four, and I was living with that woman—that's five—and then I had my promiscuous period of going to bars—that's another five; that's ten. Probably fifteen would be the total number.

2. *How many of the women were about your own age—within five years or less?*

   Oh, the majority of them. I would say perhaps ten.

3. *And how many of them were distinctly older than yourself?*

   Just two.

4. *What's the age of the oldest woman you ever had sex with?*

   45.

   How old were you then?

   I was 29.

5. *Then that means that maybe three or four women were distinctly younger than yourself?*

Yes, that's correct.

6. *And the age of the youngest?*

Would be that girl of 14.

7. *What age females do you prefer?*

About my own age.

8. *Why?*

We have common interests. I would say this has been the main reason.

B. *Male, age 30*

1. *Make a guess now as to how many different partners you've had sex with.*

I couldn't even begin to count them.

Well, is it more like 100, 1,000, 5,000, 25? What would it be?

Well, it's been a good many years. It's gotta be 1,000 males.

So you think that's your best guess?

Yeah, I think that's about right.

2. *What percentage of the males would be about your own age?*

Oh, I'd say about a quarter of them.

3. *And what percentage of the males have been distinctly older than yourself?*

Oh, the other three-quarters.

4. *What's the age of the oldest man you ever had sex with?*

I remember one guy was 72.

How old were you then?

It was last year.

5. *And none younger than yourself?*

No, I don't like that.

6. *And what's the youngest one?*

Well, I don't go for younger ones. Probably way back when I was 12 or 13, the youngest would probably have been about 15, so that would be the youngest.

7. *What age male do you prefer?*

Oh, I like them older than I.

Well, how much older?

Well, let's see. I'm 30, I like them 45 or 50.

8. *Why do you like them that age?*

Well, they take care of me. Maybe I'm looking for a father. I dunno, but they just seem more settled.

Social Position

The second block in Column II identifies the social position, including occupations, of the respondent's partners. The items in the block are as follows:

1. Students in grade school
2. Students in high school
3. Students in college
4. Students in technical or trade school
5. Clergy
6. Teachers of high school or grade school
7. College professors
8. Artists
9. Dancers or musicians
10. Professional persons
11. Business groups
12. Armed forces
13. Laboring groups
14. Law-enforcement officers
15. Percent white-collar workers
16. Percent blue-collar workers
17. Highest position held
18. Percent heterosexually married
19. Number of homosexual virgins

The interviewer may ask the respondent to indicate the major types of occupations his or her homosexual partners have had or may want to go into this more thoroughly by asking all the questions in checklist fashion. The percentages or numbers given in response to Questions 15 and 16 (partners who are either blue-collar or white-collar workers) should total 100 percent. Question 17 identifies the "biggest shot" among the respondent's partners. Question 18 asks for the percentage of respondent's homosexual partners who were heterosexually married and living with their spouses at the time they had homosexual contact with the respondent. Question 19 asks how many of the subject's partners were homosexual virgins.

The questions asked are as follows:

1. *How many of your partners were students in grade school?*

2. *How many of your partners were students in high school?*

3. *How many of your partners were students in college?*

4. *How many of your partners were students in technical or trade school?*

5. *How many of your partners were clergy?*

6. *How many of your partners were teachers?*

7. *How many of your partners were college professors?*

8. *How many of your partners were artists?*

9. *How many of your partners were dancers or musicians?*

10. *How many of your partners were professional people—lawyers, doctors, etc.?*

11. *How many of your partners were in business?*

12. *How many of your partners were in the armed forces?*

13. *How many of your partners were laborers?*

14. *How many of your partners were law-enforcement officers?*

15. *What percentage of your partners were white-collar workers?*

16. *What percentage of your partners were blue-collar workers?*

17. *What is the highest position held by any of your partners?*

18. *How many of your partners were or are heterosexually married and living with their wives (husbands)?*

19. *How many of your partners were homosexual virgins?*

Examples of Responses and Coding

A. *Female, age 35*

What have been the occupations of the various partners you've had sex with?

3,7,13,10. Well, there have been maybe five who've been college students, two college teachers, a couple of clerks, and one psychologist.

Any other occupations?

14,8,12. Yes, there was a policewoman, and an artist, and a lieutenant in the Air Force.

Any others?

That's about everyone.

What was the highest position any of your partners held?

17. Psychologist.

18. *How many women were married and living with their husbands at the time you had sex with them?*

I can remember only one.

19. *And how many were homosexual virgins?*

I think there were two.

B. *Male, age 30*

O.K. I'm sure you didn't know what some of these males did, but those that you did, what sort of occupations did they have?

Oh, mostly white-collar people. There were doctors, teachers, clerks, salesmen.

How many were blue-collar workers?

15,16. Oh, there were a few cab drivers or whatnot. I'd say 10 percent maybe. About 90 percent white-collar.

17. *What was the biggest shot you ever had sex with?*

He was a psychiatrist.

18. *What percentage of the men were married and living with their wives?*

It was a high percentage. I'd say those that I knew, maybe 20 percent.

And how many had never had a homosexual experience before the one they had with you?

None.

Relationships

Questions concerning the relationships the respondent has had with homosexual partners provide additional information about the nature of the contacts. The questions concern the following areas of information:

1. Duration of longest affair
2. Number of "oncers"
3. Initial approach
4. Relations involving love/affection
5. Percent approaches rejected
6. Any trouble from rejections

The questions, with explanations, are as follows:

1. *How long was the longest affair you've ever had with any one person?*

For several affairs, the coding would be **1 = 2y, 1 = 6m, 2 = 1y,** and so on.

2. *How many of your partners were one-night stands?*

"One-night stands" and "oncers" are people with whom the respondent had had only one homosexual contact.

3. *Who makes the initial approach?*

If the subject makes the initial approach, the response is recorded as active, **a**; if the subject always waits for the other person to make the initial approach, the recording is passive, **p**; if the approach is mutual, the recording would be mutual, **m**; and combinations of active, passive, and mutual can be recorded as **a > p, m = p,** etc.

4. *How many partners have you been in love with?*

This item does not necessarily mean that the respondent has had homosexual contact with the partner.

5. *When you make an approach, how many people reject you?*

or

What percentage of the time are you rejected?

If the respondent never makes the initial approach, then the recording would be a zero, as the question does not apply.

6. *When you have been rejected, has there ever been any trouble?*

Trouble can be identified as verbal or physical abuse, humiliation, exposure, or any perjorative insult over being rejected.

Examples of Responses and Coding

A. *Female, age 35*

1. *What's the longest affair you've ever had with a woman?*

About three years.

2. *How many women did you have just one sexual contact with and never any more?*

I can think of just one I met in a bar.

3. *When you meet a person, who makes the initial approach for homosexual relations—do you do it or does the partner do it?*

It's usually a completely mutual thing.

4. *How many women have you been in love with?*

Well, there's been a lot of infatuation and puppy love. I'd say almost fifteen of that sort, but I think what you mean, probably three.

5. *When you do the approaching, how often do you get rejected?*

Never, because I never approach until I know I'll be accepted.

B. *Male, age 30*

1. *What's the longest affair you ever had with a man?*

   Probably a year.

2. *And what percentage of your affairs were just one experience?*

   Oh, 90 percent.

3. *When you are looking for sex with a man, do you usually make the first approach, does he make it, or is it mutual?*

   No, I always let him make the first approach. I don't go after it. It's too dangerous.

4. *How many men have you been in love with?*

   There were just two that I can remember.

Racial Background

To identify the percentages of partners in various racial groups, the following questions are asked in sequence:

1. *What percentage of your partners were white?*

2. *What percentage were black?*

3. *What percentage were Oriental?*

4. *What percentage were Arab?*

5. *What percentage were American Indian?*

6. *What other races did your partners belong to?*

Examples of Responses and Coding

A. *Female, age 35*

2. *How many women with whom you had sex were black?*

   None.

3. *How many were Oriental?*

   There was one Filipino woman who was a psychologist, and the rest were white.

1,4–6. *Were there any other races than white with whom you had sex?*

   No.

B. *Male, age 30*

2. *What percentage of the men with whom you have had sex are black?*

Not very many. Maybe five men.

3. *Any Orientals?*

Yeah, a few . . . Japanese, Chinese. Not many.

6. *Other races?*

Naw.

COLUMN III: PETTING TECHNIQUES AND ORGASM

Petting Techniques

The questions in the first block of this column identify specific sexual acts that the respondent has done to partners and that have been done to the respondent by partners, as follows:

1. Maximum number of different partners in a single day
2. Group experience:
   (a) Frequencies
   (b) Ages
   (c) Number in group
   (d) Circumstances
   (e) Techniques
3. Lip kissing (passive, active)
4. Tongue kissing (passive, active)
5. Kissing body (passive, active)
6. Breast manipulation—manual (passive, active)
7. Breast manipulation—oral (passive, active)
8. Genitalia manipulation—manual (passive, active)
9. Genitalia manipulation—oral (passive, active)
10. Scrotum manipulation—manual (male only; passive, active)
11. Scrotum manipulation—oral (male only; passive, active)
12. Anus manipulation—manual (passive, active)
13. Anus manipulation—oral (passive, active)
14. Bondage (passive, active)
15. Flagellation (passive, active)

The vertical line dividing this block (see Figure 29–2) accommodates Questions 3 through 15 in both active and passive sequence. The questions may be asked concurrently—that is, for passive behavior and active behavior at the same time—or they may be asked in sequence, with all passive behavior covered first and then all active behavior. The questions include not only petting techniques but also group experience and maximum number of different partners in a single day.

The questions are asked in the following form:

1. *What is the highest number of different partners you have ever had in a single day?*

2. *What group experience have you had?*

    (a) How frequently have you experienced homosexual group sex?

    (b) What age were you during these experiences?

    (c) How many people were involved in the groups?

    (d) Under what circumstances did the group experience occur?

    (e) What techniques were used?

Questions 3 through 15 may be posed in a telling fashion rather than an asking fashion in the following way:

PASSIVE

3. *Your partner kisses you?*

4. *Your partner tongue kisses you?*

5. *Your partner kisses your body?*

6. (males) *There's hand on your nipple?*

    (females) *There's hand on your breast?*

7. (males) *There's mouth on your nipple?*

    (females) *There's mouth on your breast?*

8. (males) *There's hand on your penis?*

    (females) *There's hand on your genitals (or sex organ)?*

9. (males) *There's mouth on your penis?*

10. (males) *Partner's hand on your scrotum?*

11. (males) *Partner's mouth on your scrotum?*

12. *Partner's hand on your anus?*

13. *Partner's mouth on your anus?*

14. *Are you tied, bound, or chained?*

15. *Are you whipped or beaten in any way?*

ACTIVE

3. *You kiss your partner?*

4. *You tongue kiss your partner?*

5. *You kiss your partner's body?*

6. (males) *Your hand on your partner's nipple?*

   (females) *Your hand on your partner's breast?*

7. *Your mouth on your partner's nipple?*

8. (males) *Your hand on your partner's penis?*

   (females) *Your hand on your partner's genitals (or sex organ)?*

9. (males) *Your mouth on your partner's penis?*

10. (males) *Your hand on your partner's scrotum?*

11. (males) *Your mouth on your partner's scrotum?*

12. *Your hand on your partner's anus?*

13. *Your mouth on your partner's anus?*

14. *Do you bind, tie, or chain your partner?*

15. *Do you whip or beat your partner?*

Examples of Responses and Coding

A. *Female, age 35*

1. *What is the highest number of partners you've had in any one day?*

   One.

2. *Have you had any sexual contact where there were more than two of you to-gether at the same time?*

   No, I've never done that.

3. *While having sex with women, there's kissing?*

   Yes.

4. *Tongue kissing?*

   Oh, yes.

5. *Is there kissing the entire body?*

   Yes.

6. *And their hand on your breasts?*

   Sure.

7. *And mouth on breast?*

   Sure.

9. *And their mouth on your genitalia?*

Sure.

3-9. *And do you do the same with them?*

Yes, that's right.

(It is safe to assume there has been hand on genitalia if there has been oral sex.)

12. *Is there any stimulation of the anus?*

No.

14. *Has there been any masochism, where you've had the women bind you or beat you or spank you?*

No, I haven't been interested in that.

Has there been any sadism?

One time one woman wanted that, but I refused to do it, and that broke up our relationship.

B. *Male, age 30*

1. *What's the most number of partners you've had in a single day?*

Five, I guess, would be the maximum.

And have you had group experiences, where there have been more than two of you together?

Oh yeah, that's happened.

How often, do you suppose?

2. (*a* and *d*) Oh maybe ten times. I go to the baths . . . oh no, it's gotta be twenty times. I go to the baths.

2. *(b) How old were you the first time you had more than one male at a time?*

About 21.

2. *(c) What's been the biggest group you've had?*

About ten men, I guess.

3. *When you have sex with men, do they kiss?*

Yes.

4. *Do they tongue kiss?*

Sure.

5. *Kiss your body?*

Yeah, sometimes.

8. *Do they put their hand on your cock?*

Sure.

9. *And their mouth on your cock?*

Sure.

10. *And their hand on your bag?*

Yeah, sometimes.

11. *And their mouth on your bag?*

Sure, that happens.

13. *Do they rim?*

Sure.

And do you do all this to them, the same way?

Yes, it's pretty much give and take.

Have you ever had any of the men tie you up or spank you or beat you?

No, I don't go for that shit.

And have any of the men ever wanted you to do that to them?

No. I had a golden shower once where I urinated on a boy, but I don't care for that.

Partner Orgasm

Questions concerning partner orgasm identify orgasm in varieties of techniques as follows:

1. Percent orgasm in homosexual relations
2. Percent in masturbation
3. Percent oral-genital
4. Percent ejaculate
5. Percent finger/hand in anus
6. Percent anal intercourse
7. Percent other techniques

The questions are asked as follows:

1. *What percentage of the time do your partners come to climax in homosexual relations?*

2. *What percentage of the time do they come by your masturbating them?*

3. *What percentage of the time do they come by your having oral sex with them?*

4. *Do you swallow or spit out the semen?*

5. *What percentage of the time do your partners come to climax by your finger or hand manipulation in their anus?*

6. *What percentage of the time do your partners come to orgasm in anal intercourse with you?*

7. *What percentage of the time are other techniques used for partner orgasm?*

Examples of Responses and Coding

A. *Female, age 35*

1. *Now, when you have sex with females, what percentage of the time do your partners have orgasms?*

I'd say close to 100 percent of the time.

2. *And of the sex you've had with women, what percentage has been by your masturbating them?*

Well, in the past, that was the usual way, but now it occurs very much less often, because I'm mostly into oral sex, so the oral sex would be 90 percent of it now, and masturbation 5 percent, and rubbing our bodies together 5 percent.

B. *Male, age 30*

1. *What percentage of the time do the other men come when you have sex with them?*

Oh, I'd say about 80 percent of the time.

2,3,5,6. *And when they come, is it more often by your going down on them, or your masturbating them, or by their having intercourse with you?*

Well, I don't like anal intercourse. It's mostly by my going down on them. It's very rarely by my masturbating them.

4. *Do you spit out the come?*

Yeah, unless I'm in love.

Subject Orgasm

Eight questions in Column III are concerned with the respondent's orgasm. The questions asked are as follows:

1. *What percentage of the time do you have orgasm in a homosexual encounter?*

2. *Have you ever come spontaneously, just by the fact that the other person has come?*

3. *What percentage of the time do you come just by being masturbated?*

4. *(males) What percentage of the time do you come by having your penis sucked?*

(females) What percentage of the time do you come by having your sex organs sucked?

5. *What percentage of the time do you come by having fingers or a hand stimulate your anus, externally or internally?*

6. *What percentage of the time do you come in anal intercourse?*

7. *What percentage of the time do you come by full body contact?*

8. *What percentage of the time do you come in other techniques?*

Examples of Responses and Coding

A. *Female, age 35*

1. *And you always have orgasm?*

Yes, essentially always.

2. *Have you ever come spontaneously, just by the fact that the other person comes?*

No, I can't remember that.

4. *And most of the time you come it's by oral sex, is that correct?*

Yes, I'd say 90 percent of the time. And 5 percent by masturbation, and 5 percent by body contact.

B. *Male, age 30*

1. *Do you always come?*

Yes, I always come.

2. *Do you ever come spontaneously, just by the fact that they've come?*

Oh, that's happened two or three times.

4,6. *And do you come mostly by screwing them, or by their going down on you?*

I'd say it's mostly by their giving me head—80 percent—and most of the rest by screwing them, and not very often by their masturbating me.

5. *Ever by fist fucking?*

No.

Demographics of Orgasm

The last questions in Column III contain an assortment of items that provide additional insight into the respondent's homosexual experience. The questions asked are as follows:

1. *Does the odor or taste of semen (or female genitalia) arouse you sexually?*

2. *What percentage of the time do you experience simultaneous orgasm with your partner?*

3. *What percent of the time do you experience consecutive orgasms with your partner?*

4. *What percent of the time do your experiences occur in the light?*

    and

    What percent of the time do your experiences occur in the dark?

5. *What percent of the time do your experiences occur in the nude?*

    and

    What percent of the time do your experiences occur with clothing on?

6. *In what places do your experiences occur?*

A checklist of places for Question 6 would include the respondent's home, the partner's home, another friend's home, a car, outdoors, in a park, a bar, a bath, on a plane, a train, on water, in water, on the beach, and so on.

Examples of Responses and Coding

A. *Female, age 35*

1. *Did the smell of the woman's vagina arouse you sexually?*

    Hmm. I never thought about that. It didn't turn me off but I don't think it aroused me.

2,3. *Do you usually come together, or first one and then the other?*

    Well, 69 doesn't work. Usually it's consecutive rather than simultaneous, and I like it better that way.

4. *Do you have it in the light or dark?*

    Dim light, mostly.

5. *Are your clothes all on or clothes off?*

    Oh, yes, clothes all off.

6. *What different places have you had homosexual contact?*

Sometimes where we've lived together, sometimes at the other woman's home, sometimes in my apartment.

Ever any other place?

No, I can't think of any other place.

B. *Male, age 30*

1. *You say you spit out semen. How do you feel about the taste of come?*

Oh, I don't care for it.

2,3. *Do you usually come in 69 together, or first one and then the other?*

No, it's usually first one and then the other. I don't like 69.

4. *Do you like it in the light or dark?*

I don't care.

5. *Do you like it with your clothes on or off?*

Clothes off.

6. *Where have you had sex with men—what different places?*

Oh, their apartment, my apartment, tearooms, out on the beach, baths. Those are mostly where it is.

COLUMN IV: PARTNER PREFERENCES AND SOURCES OF CONTACTS

Partner Preferences

Questions in the first block of Column IV are concerned with the respondent's preferences for masculine or feminine types of partners, partners of particular height, weight, complexion, with particular amounts of body hair or smooth, hairless bodies, particular genital or breast characteristics, circumcised or uncircumcised partners, and other physical or psychological qualities as follows:

1. Prefer masculine or feminine partners
2. Preferred height
3. Preferred weight
4. Preferred complexion
5. Body hair
6. Penis size (males only)
7. Scrotum (males only)
8. Circumcision (males only)
9. Why preference
10. Breasts (females only)
11. Personality
12. Intelligence
13. Dress
14. Body language and appearance
15. Other preferences, e.g., cultural aspects, etc.

The questions asked in sequence are:

1. *Do you prefer your homosexual partners to be more masculine or feminine?*

2. *Do you prefer your partners tall, medium, or short, or don't you care?*

3. *Do you prefer your partners light, heavy, medium, or don't you care?*

4. *Do you prefer your partner's complexion to be light, dark, in between, or don't you care?*

5. *Do you prefer your partner to have a smooth body, a hairy body, or do you care?*

6. (males only) *Do you prefer a small penis, a large penis, a medium-size penis, or do you care?*

7. (males only) *Do you prefer a scrotum that is medium size, small, or large, or do you care?*

8. (males only) *Do you prefer your partner to be circumcised or not circumcised, or does it make any difference?*

9. (males only) *Why do you prefer penises circumcised (or uncircumcised)?*

10. (females only) *Are there particular breast characteristics that you prefer?*

11. *Are there particular personalities that you have a preference for?*

12. *Do you prefer partners who are dumb, average, intelligent, or does it matter?*

13. *Have you a preference for styles of dress in your partners?*

14. *What body language and general appearance do you prefer your partners to have?*

15. *Are there any other physical qualities or other preferences, such as cultural aspects, that you prefer in a partner?*

Examples of Responses and Coding

A. *Female, age 35*

1. *Do you prefer women who are more masculine or more feminine?*
   I think more feminine.

2. *Do you like them tall, medium, short, or don't you care?*
   I really don't care.

3. *Do you like them heavy, medium, light, or don't you care?*
   Oh, I don't want them too fat. I'd say medium.

4. *Do you like them light-skinned, dark-skinned?*
   It really doesn't make any difference.

5. *Do you like them to have hair on their body or not?*

I like smooth skin.

10. *Do you prefer their breasts to be small, medium, or large?*

I just don't care.

Are there any other particular qualities about women that you like?

11-15. Well, I like them cultured, intelligent, and with a good sense of humor.

13. *Do you care about how they dress?*

Neat and feminine.

B. *Male, age 30*

1. *Do you prefer a man who is more masculine or more feminine?*

More masculine.

2. *Do you like them tall, medium, or short?*

I like them tall.

3. *Do you like them heavy, medium, or light?*

I really don't care, as long as they're not too fat.

4. *Do you like them light-skinned or dark-skinned?*

I don't care.

5. *Do you like them to have hair on their body or not?*

Yes, I like hairy men.

6. *Do you like their penises to be small, medium, or large?*

Oh, large penises. I like big cocks. I'm a size queen, I guess.

7. *Do you like their bag to be small, medium, or large?*

Yes, I like that to be big too.

8. *Do you like them to be circumcised or not?*

Yeah, circumcised.

9. *Why?*

It's cleaner that way.

11-15. *What other characteristics about men appeal to you?*

I like them rough, assertive, and strong.

13. *Do you care how they dress?*

Like men.

Sources of Contacts

Questions about the sources of contacts for homosexual activities are concerned with two issues: (1) the percentage of contacts who have been introduced versus those who have been picked up and (2) the sources at which these contacts were made. The interview uses a checklist of places, covering the following items:

1. Percent introduced	16. Bus
2. Percent pick-ups	17. Train
3. Street	18. Plane
4. Hotel lobbies	19. Boat/ship
5. Theatres	20. Public baths
6. Parks	21. Gay baths
7. Bars/clubs	22. Discos
8. Gay bars/clubs	23. Church
9. Beach	24. University campus
10. Hitchhiking	25. Dormitory
11. Railroad stations	26. YMCA/YWCA
12. Bus stations	(YMHA/YWHA)
13. Airports	27. Restaurant
14. Public toilets	28. Resort
15. Subways	29. Other

Responses to Questions 1 and 2, regarding the percentage of partners who were introduced and picked up, should total 100 percent. Questions 3 through 29 identify places where the respondent was picked up or picked up somebody else, and include partners who were introduced to the respondent just prior to the homosexual activities. Places of contact include both passive and active behavior of the respondent. The questions asked are as follows:

1. *What percentage of your partners were introduced to you by friends or other people?*

2. *What percentage of your partners were pick-ups?*

Answers to Questions 3 through 29 may be recorded in any way the interviewer finds easiest. The question asked is as follows:

How many of your partners were picked up—

3. *on the street?*

4. *in a hotel lobby?*

5. *in a theatre?*

6. *in a park?*

7. *in a bar or club?*

   8. *in a gay bar or club?*

   9. *on the beach?*

  10. *hitchhiking?*

  11. *in a railway station?*

  12. *bus station?*

  13. *airport?*

  14. *public toilet?*

  15. *subway?*

  16. *on a bus?*

  17. *on a train?*

  18. *on a plane?*

  19. *on a boat/ship?*

  20. *in a public bath?*

  21. *in a gay bath?*

  22. *in a disco?*

  23. *in a church or synagogue?*

  24. *on a university campus?*

  25. *in a dormitory residence?*

  26. *YMCA or YWCA?*

  27. *in a restaurant?*

  28. *in a resort facility?*

  29. *what other places?*

Examples of Responses and Coding

A. *Female, age 35*

  1. *What percentage of your partners were introduced to you by others?*

      Oh, the majority of them.

2, 8. *You mentioned the fact that there was a part of your life when you were going to gay bars. How many women did you pick up at gay bars?*

      Oh, there were only three.

      Have you ever been picked up or picked up a woman anyplace else, like on the street, or in a movie, or in a park?

      No, I can't think of any other place.

B. *Male, age 30*

  1. *What percentage of the men you've had sex with have been pick-ups in one way or another?*

  90 percent.

  2. *So about 10 percent of them through introduction?*

  Yes.

3, 6. *Where have they picked you up?*

  Sometimes on the streets, in parks.

  4. *In hotels?*

  No, not there.

  5. *In movies?*

  Once in a long time.

  7. *Bars?*

  Oh, sure.

  9. *On the beach?*

  Yeah.

  10. *Hitchhiking?*

  Yeah, when I was younger.

11, 12. *Railroad stations or bus terminals?*

  Yeah, occasionally.

16, 17. *On a bus or train?*

  No, I don't remember that happening.

  21. *At the baths?*

  Yeah.

  Additional places may be asked if this seems appropriate.

COLUMN V: SOCIAL CONFLICTS AND INDICATORS

Social Conflicts

The twelve questions on the social conflicts related to homosexuality are concerned primarily with the difficulties the respondent has met in home, school, community, and business. Additional questions center on penal history, blackmail, and robbery, both active and passive, as a result of homosexual behavior. The items covered are:

1. Difficulties in grade school
2. Difficulties in high school
3. Difficulties in college, trade, technical
4. Difficulties in community
5. Difficulties in work or business
6. Difficulties with parents
7. Do parents know?
8. (a) conflict with police
   (b) Number of arrests
   (c) Court action
   (d) Outcome and penal history
9. (a) Blackmail—passive
   (b) Blackmail—active
10. (a) Robbery—passive
    (b) Robbery—active
11. Gay bars or clubs
12. Percent gay associates

The questions asked are as follows:

1. *Did you ever get into any trouble over homosexuality while you were in grade school?*

2. *Did you ever get into trouble over homosexuality while you were in high school?*

3. *While you were in college (trade or technical school)?*

4. *In your local community?*

5. *In you place of business or work?*

6. *With your parents?*

7. *Do your parents know about your homosexuality?*

8. *(a) Have you been in any trouble with the police over homosexuality?*

   (b) How many times have you been arrested as a result of homosexual behavior?

   (c) What court action was taken?

   (d) What was the outcome?

9. *(a) Have you ever been blackmailed because of homosexuality?*

   (b) Have you ever blackmailed anyone because of his or her homosexuality

10. *(a) Have you ever been rolled or robbed in a homosexual relation?*

    (b) Have you ever rolled or robbed anyone in a homosexual relation that you were participating in?

11. *Do you frequent gay bars or clubs?*

12. *What percent of your friends are gay?*

Examples of Responses and Coding

A. *Female, age 35*

   What trouble have you gotten into over your homosexuality?

   Well, really not any trouble at all.

1–3. *I'm thinking of in school, for example. Like in high school or college?*

No, not at all.

4. *Any trouble in your community?*

No.

5. *Any trouble where you work?*

No, I assume they know I'm gay at work, and it doesn't seem to make any difference.

8. *Any trouble with the police?*

None at all.

7. *How about with your parents?*

Oh, a little trouble. I told them about it when I was in college, and they were very disappointed, but they have pretty much accepted it now. In fact, I even brought a girlfriend home one time, and they accepted her.

9. *Have you ever been blackmailed over homosexuality?*

No, I haven't.

10. *Ever been robbed?*

No.

Ever robbed anyone?

No.

11. *Do you go to gay bars?*

Yes, sometimes.

12. *What percent of your friends are gay?*

About three-fourths.

B. *Male, age 30*

1. *What trouble have you gotten into over homosexuality?*

Any trouble in grade school?

No.

2. *In high school?*

Yes, they found out about it, and the guys used to kid me about it in high school.

3. *And you never went to college?*

No.

4. *Ever in your community?*

No, I don't think so.

5. *In your business?*

Yeah, I've lost a couple of jobs because of homosexuality.

6, 7. *Any trouble with your parents?*

No. I haven't seen my parents for a long time, and they don't know anything about me.

8. *Trouble with the police?*

Yes. One time I was arrested in a gay bar when they had a raid. I spent overnight in jail, and then they released me.

9. *(a) Have you ever been blackmailed?*

No.

(b) Have you ever blackmailed anybody?

Yes, one guy I shook down for $100 once, because I would have told on him if he hadn't come through with it.

10. *(a) Have you ever been rolled?*

No.

(b) Have you ever rolled anybody?

Yeah, two or three times I've lifted some money off a guy when he was drunk.

11. (Already answered)

12. *What percent of your friends are gay?*

About half.

Homosexual Indicators

The second block of questions in Column V is concerned with physical characteristics that may or may not be indicators of a person's homosexuality. The questions are for both the subject and the interviewer. The two sets of responses are recorded on both sides of the column, divided by the vertical line as shown in Figure 29-2, with the subjects responses—that is, the respondent's recognition of physical movements or characteristics that may be homosexual stigmatizing—recorded to the left of the line. At the same time, the interviewer evaluates the respondent and records his or her own perceptions on the right side of the column. To clarify further, as the interviewer asks each of the questions, he should judge the respondent on each of the items and make an evaluation—e.g., whether the interviewer thinks the various characteristics are obvious. These perceptions are coded and recorded on the right side of the column while the respondent's self-perceptions are coded and recorded on the left side of the column.

The questions are asked only about the respondent, not about his or her partners, and are concerned with whether the respondent thinks he or she is obvious in interjecting homosexual orientation in public or private. A general question is asked:

If you could see yourself walking down the street, is there any way you could tell you were homosexual?

Specifically, the following may be asked:

1. *By the way you move your hands?*

2. *By the way you swing your hips?*

3. *By the way you speak?*

4. *By the way you dress?*

5. *Do you dress in drag?*

6. *Do you crossdress in private?*

7. *By the way you wear your hair?*

8. *Do you pluck your eyebrows?*

9. *By the way you walk?*

10. *Do you wear make-up?*

11. *By the way you move your head?*

12. *Are there any other ways that would tell someone else of your homosexual behavior?*

Examples of Responses and Coding

A. *Female, age 35*

If you could see yourself walking down the street, is there any way you could tell that you are a lesbian?

I don't think so.

1. *How about the way you move your hands?*

No.

9. *The way you walk?*

No.

3. *How about your voice?*

No, I think it's very average.

4. *How about the way you dress?*

Well, I like to dress unisexually, but everybody does now, so I don't think . . . it might . . . well, maybe that would give me away a little bit.

5. *Do you ever dress mannishly?*

No.

7. *How about the way you wear your hair?*

Well, it seems to be a little short. But a lot of women have short hair. No, I don't think that would do it.

B. *Male, age 30*

If you were to see yourself walking down the street, is there any way you could tell that you are a homosexual?

No, there isn't a thing I can think of.

1. *Nothing about the way you move your hands?*

No.

2, 9. *The way you walk or the way you sway your hips.*

No.

3. *Your voice?*

No.

4. *The way you dress?*

No.

5. *Have you ever gone in drag?*

No.

7. *The way you wear your hair?*

No.

8. *Do you pluck your eyebrows?*

No.

COLUMN VI: PROSTITUTION AND SELF-PERCEPTION

Prostitution

The first block in this column is concerned with both the subject as a prostitute and the subject as a customer of prostitutes. Information tapped includes the following:

1. Ever given *gifts*
2. Ever received *gifts*
3. Ever been paid, amount
4. Frequency
5. Paid a prostitute, amount
6. Frequency
7. Ever been kept, duration
8. Ever kept a homosexual, duration

The questions asked are:

1. *Have you ever given gifts in a homosexual relationship?*

2. *Have you ever received gifts in a homosexual relationship?*

3. *Have you ever been paid cash for homosexual behavior?*

   What were the amounts paid?

4. *How frequently have you been paid for homosexual activities?*

5. *Have you ever paid a homosexual prostitute?*

   What amounts did you pay?

6. *How frequently did you pay a homosexual prostitute?*

7. *Have you ever been kept?*

   For how long?

8. *Have you ever kept a homosexual?*

   For how long?

Examples of Responses and Coding

A. *Female, age 35*

1, 2. *Have you ever given gifts or received gifts as part of a homosexual relationship?*

No, we give gifts, but not because of homosexuality.

3. *Have you ever been paid for it?*

No, I haven't.

7. *Have you ever been kept?*

No, I guess not.

8. *Have you ever kept a woman?*

Well, the woman I lived with didn't have a very good job, so I paid most of the expenses.

B. *Male, age 30*

2. *Have you ever received any gifts for homosexual relations?*

No, I can't remember that.

1. *Or given gifts?*

No.

4. *How often have you been paid for homosexual relations?*

Oh, I've hustled some. Back when I was younger. I don't do it any more.

3. *How much were you paid?*

Ten or twenty dollars.

5. *Have you ever paid for it?*

No.

7. *Have you ever been kept by a man?*

Yes, I've been kept several times for short periods of time.

8. *Have you ever kept a man?*

No.

Self-Perception

Questions in this block are concerned with the subject's self-analysis of homosexual behavior, as follows:

1. (a) Subject's rating on 0-6 scale
   (b) Interviewer's rating on 0-6 scale
2. Regret
3. Why (conflicts)
4. Expectancy to continue

5. Expectancy to change
6. Can you change
7. Want gay marriage
8. Recommendation to others
9. Factors account for *your* H

The items cover conflicts and regrets, expectancy for continuation, expectancy for transfer to heterosexual orientation, recommendation of homosexuality for others, a self-rating of the subject's degree of homosexuality on a 0-6 scale (developed by Kinsey and called the Kinsey 0-6 scale), the interpreter's rating, and the subject's analysis of factors that account for his or her homosexuality. The 0-6 scale is based on both overt behavior and psychological response, as follows:

0   persons who are exclusively heterosexual, both overtly and psychologically

1   persons who are primarily heterosexual and only incidentally homosexual

2   persons who are both heterosexual and homosexual but more heterosexual

3   persons who are both heterosexual and homosexual and have no preference for one or the other

4   persons who are both homosexual and heterosexual but more homosexual

5   persons who are primarily homosexual and only incidentally heterosexual

6   persons who are exclusively homosexual

The questions asked are:

1. *(a) Where would you rate yourself on the 0–6 scale?*

   (b) The interviewer records his or her own perception of the respondent.

2. *Have you ever regretted your homosexual history?*

3. *Why have you regretted it?*

4. *Will you continue with your homosexuality in the future?*

5. *Have you ever wanted to change?*

6. *If you wanted to, could you change?*

7. *Have you ever wanted to marry someone of the opposite sex and live as husband and wife?*

8. *Suppose a young boy or girl came to you who had just started having homosexual relations and wanted your advice as to whether or not he or she should continue. What would you tell him or her?*

9. *What do you see as factors which account for your own homosexuality?*

If the respondent is not familiar with the Kinsey 0–6 scale, it must be explained to her or him before Question 1 is asked.

Examples of Responses and Coding

A. *Female, age 35*

1. *How would you rate yourself on the 0–6 scale?*

   Well, I know the scale, and I'm quite sure that I would be a 6 overtly, and probably a 5 psychologically.

2, 3. *Have you ever regretted being homosexual?*

   Well, I like children. I sort of regret that I'm not going to have any, but that isn't really regretting homosexuality. No, I don't think I have.

4. *You'll continue with homosexuality?*

   Oh, yes.

5. *Have you wanted to change?*

   No, I haven't.

6. *Do you think you could change if you wanted to?*

Probably not now.

8. *Supposing a young girl came to you who had just started having homosexual relations, and she wanted your advice as to whether she should continue or not. What would you tell her?*

I wouldn't give her advice. I'd tell her to try it, and if she liked it, fine, and if she didn't, give it up.

9. *Why do you think you have a homosexual history?*

Well, I've thought about this a great deal, and I can't come up with any ideas at all. I got along with my parents, and we got along with each other, and I like males as friends. I don't think that early experience at 14 had any effect, cause I was very interested in it then. So I really don't know.

B. *Male, age 30*

1. *How would you rate yourself on the 0–6 scale?*

I'm probably a 5, maybe a 4.

2. *Have you ever regretted having homosexual relations?*

No.

4. *You'll continue?*

Yes.

5. *Have you wanted to change?*

No, I'm happy with my life.

6. *Do you think you could change?*

Sure I could, if I wanted to.

7. *Did you ever want to marry a woman and live as man and wife?*

No, not at all.

8. *Suppose a young boy came to you who had started having homosexual relations and wanted your advice as to whether he should continue or not. What would you tell him?*

I'd tell him to go ahead. It's fun.

9. *Why do you think that you have developed a homosexual life?*

Well, it's a lot easier, it's more fun, you don't have to get hassled by women, and I think maybe I've been looking for a father that I didn't have and a benefactor. I can't think of anything else.

I	II	III	IV	V		
			GROUP SEX	SOCIAL-SEXUAL		
FIRST EXPERIENCE	AGES AND RELATIONSHIPS			BACKGROUND AND ATTITUDES		
		PETTING TECHNIQUES (ACTIVE)				
FREQUENCIES			EXHIBITIONISM			
	OCCUPATIONS					
			INCOME FROM PROSTITUTION			
		PETTING TECHNIQUES (PASSIVE)				
			SOCIAL INVOLVEMENTS			
	RACIAL GROUPS					
		RATE OF ORGASM	PROPHYLAXIS AND CONTRACEPTION			
	SOURCES OF CONTACTS					
		POSITIONS				

FIGURE 30-1

30

Prostitution Inventory

The Prostitution Inventory was developed as a separate schedule of questions to tap data on the professional life of prostitutes. Like those with extensive homosexual histories, people involved professionally in prostitution have a lifestyle, vocabulary, and way of looking at their environment different from those of other people. As a result, they have quite different experiences. Again, prostitution is defined as receiving money in exchange for intercourse or other sexual activities from partners chosen on a relatively undiscriminating basis. (Although there is male homosexual prostitution, a limited amount of male heterosexual prostitution, and even a minuscule amount of female homosexual prostitution, we are concerned here only with female heterosexual prostitution.) It is permissible to record percentages rather than discreet numbers, and the interviewer should record responses in whatever form the subject offers.

The Prostitution Inventory occupies five columns of a grid the same size as the Sex History Inventory. Figure 30-1 identifies the blocks of information sought in the inventory. Figure 30-2 shows where responses to the various questions are recorded. Those who wish to expand the inventory for special purposes may use additional columns.

The information sought is a description of the first experience in prostitution and frequencies of intercourse during the first year of prostitution (Column I); ages, relationships, occupations, racial groups, and sources of contacts of the prostitute's partners (Column II); the petting techniques—both active and passive—used by the prostitute and the partner, the rate of orgasm with partners, and positions (Column III); group activities, exhibitionism, income, social involvements, prophylaxis and contraception (Column IV); and sociosexual background and attitudes (Column V).

FIGURE 30-2

I	II	III	IV	V
1	1	1	1	1
2	2	2	2	2
3	3	3	3	3
4	4	4	4	4
	5	5	5	5
	6	6	6	6
	7	7		7
		8	7	8
	8	9	8	9
	9	10	9	
	10	11	10	
	11	12	11	
	12	13	12	
5	13	14		
6	14	15		
7	15		13	
8	16	16	14	
9	17	17	15	
	18	18	16	
	19	19	17	
	20	20	18	
	21	21	19	
		22	20	
	22	23	21	
	23	24		
	24	25		
		26	22	
	25		23	
	26	27	24	
	27	28	25	
	28	29		
		30		
	29	31	26	
	30	32	27	
	31	33	28	
	32		29	
	33		30	
	34			
	35			

These areas are grouped sequentially to allow for an easy flow of the interview and to provide structure within which the interviewer can rapidly establish rapport with the subject.

COLUMN I

First Experience

In the first block of Column I, the following information is sought:

1. Age at first paid intercourse
2. Partner's age
3. Circumstances
4. Amount paid

The questions, asked individually, are as follows:

1. *How old were you the first time you turned a trick?*

2. *What age was your partner?*

3. *Tell me what happened?*

4. *How much money did you receive?*

Frequencies First Year

The rest of Column I is concerned with frequencies of heterosexual prostitution. As in the homosexual inventory, the first year of prostitution activity is singled out as something rather special. It is a period of activity that is easier to remember than are subsequent years.

The questions, asked in sequence, are:

5. *How often did you turn tricks during that first year?*

6. *What is the largest number of tricks you ever turned in any one day?*

7. *What is the largest number of tricks you've ever turned in any single week?*

8. *What is the average number of tricks you turned in a day?*

9. *What is the average number of tricks you turned in a week?*

Examples of Responses and Coding

A. *Female, age 35, prostitute, never married, first experience (see Figure 30-3 for coding of Column I responses)*

1. *Okay, when was the first trick you ever turned?*

   I was 17.

2. *How old was he?*

   About 25.

FIGURE 30-3

I				
17				
25 ±				
To bar w Pr				
$10 frnd.				
She intro				
John				
His place.				
3x				
25/d				
35/				
3/d 5/d 31-33				
15/ 25/ 31-33				

3. *Tell me what happened that first time.*

Well, I was out of high school, looking for a job, and one of my girlfriends who's in the life suggested I make some easy money. So I went along with this and she introduced me to a john in a bar and he suggested that we go to his place and that was my first trick.

4. *How much did he pay you?*

Well, I was so stupid then that I didn't get money up front, and he finally gave me $10 after a big hassle at the end.

B. *Female, age 35, frequencies first year*

O.K. *You've been in the life now about eighteen years. Is that right?*
Yes.

5. *And how often did you turn tricks that first year?*

I didn't really get started till I was 18. It was only three times at 17.

6. *What's the most you ever turned in a day?*

Well, there was a convention here once and, my God, I was flat on my back all day—I must have turned twenty-five tricks that day.

7. *And what do you suppose the maximum in a week has been?*

Probably thirty-five in a week.

How many days a week do you usually work?

I usually take two days off a week. (Confirms five-day work week.)

8. *How many tricks a day do you average?*

I suppose it's about three.

Has that been true ever since you were 18?

No, when I worked in a house it averaged five a day. For the rest of the time I guess you could say three a day is about right.

When did you work in a house?

For three years starting when I was 31.

9. *That means you turn about fifteen tricks a week.*

Yeah, that sounds about right.

COLUMN II

Information in the second column gives an overview of the nature of the partners with whom the prostitute has had contact. Information is divided into five areas: age of partners and their relation to the respondent, education levels, occupations, racial groups and sources of contact. Each of these areas has a checklist of individually numbered questions that the interviewer can ask in sequential order.

Ages and Relationships

In the first block of Column II, the following information is sought (Figure 30–2 shows where these data are recorded):

1. *What is the age of the oldest trick you ever turned?*

   What is the age of the youngest trick you ever turned?

2. *How old were most of your tricks?*

3. *What percent of your tricks do you see more than one time?*

4. *What's the longest time you have ever seen the same trick?*

5. *What percent of your tricks were married?*

6. *How many of your tricks do you really get to like a lot?*

7. *How many of your tricks had never had intercourse until they had it with you? Do you like virgins?*

Example of Responses and Coding

Female, age 35 (see Figure 30–4 for coding of Column II responses)

1. *What's the age of the oldest trick you ever turned?*

   He was in his seventies, about 75.

   And what's the youngest trick you ever turned?

   Probably 16.

2. *What do you suppose is the age of the average trick?*

   Oh, about 40.

3. *What percentage of them come back to you more than once?*

   I had some regular customers. I'd say 65 percent come back.

4. *What's the longest period of time any one trick kept coming back to you?*

   About two years.

5. *What percentage of your tricks are married, do you suppose?*

   Oh, I'd say the biggest percentage, maybe 80 percent.

FIGURE 30-4

	II			
	15-16			
	40			
	65%			
	2y			
	80%			
	3-4			
	X X			
	X			
	3-4			
	30			
	X			
	5-6			
	30-40			
	X			
	10			
	4-5			
	—			
	—			
	✓			
	5			
	✓✓			
	Jdge			
	80			
	20			
	90			
	10			
	10-12			
	X			
	—			
	X			
	3y			
	10y			
	Most			
	X			
	5y			

6. *And how often do you really get some mutual esteem from your tricks, where you really like each other as individuals?*

I'm telling you, not very often. Maybe it's happened three or four times.

7. *How many tricks were virgins, that is, had never had intercourse with a woman before until they had been with you?*

I don't recall any.

Do you like virgins?

Not particularly.

Occupations

There are seventeen questions concerning the occupations of the partners who have paid the prostitute for intercourse. These are administered as a checklist, to get a picture of the socioeconomic status of the prostitute's customers. Again, responses are based on the prostitute's knowledge or perception of the partner's status. *All* of the questions should be asked. They may be phrased as follows:

8. *How many tricks were going to grade school at the time you had intercourse with them?*

9. *How many were in high school?*

10. *How many were in college?*

11. *How many of your tricks were grade school or high school teachers?*

12. *How many were college teachers?*

13. *How many were M.D.s?*

14. *How many were dentists?*

15. *How many were lawyers?*

16. *How many were clergymen?*

17. *How many were professional actors? Actresses?*

18. *How many were artists?*

19. *How many were musicians?*

20. *How many were writers?*

21. *How many were business executives?*

22. *What's the most prestigious occupation or the "biggest shot" you ever got paid to have intercourse with?*

23. *What percent of your tricks were white-collar workers?*

24. *What percent of your tricks were blue-collar workers or laborers?*

Example of Responses and Coding

Female, age 35, never married

8. *How many of your tricks were in grade school at the time?*

   (This question has already been answered because her youngest trick was 16.)

9. *How many of your tricks were in high school at the time?*

   Very few, maybe three or four.

10. *How many were college students?*

    Oh, lots of them. Maybe thirty or so.

11. *How many teachers, grade school or high school teachers?*
    Don't remember any of those.

12. *College professors?*

    Oh, five or six maybe.

13. *How many were M.D.s?*

    Uh, lots of M.D.s, maybe thirty or forty.

14. *Any dentists?*

    No, I can't remember them.

15. *Lawyers?*

    Oh yeah, lots of lawyers, another ten maybe.

16. *How many were clergymen?*

    Oh, I've had my share of ministers, maybe four or five.

17. *Any professional actors?*

    A few.

18. *Any professional artists, painters?*

    Yeah, a few.

19. *Musicians?*

    Yeah, lots. I can't remember how many.

20. *Writers?*

    Maybe five.

21. *Business executives?*

Most of them.

22. *What's the biggest shot you ever turned a trick with?*

He was a judge.

23, 24. *What percentage were white-collar people versus blue-collar people?*

Oh, mostly white-collar, they're the ones that have the money. I would say 80 percent were white-collar and 20 percent were blue-collar.

Racial Groups

These questions are designed to determine the racial backgrounds of the respondent's customers. They can also be expanded to include ethnic group percentages.

Example of Responses and Coding

Female, age 35

25. *What percentage of your tricks are white?*

90 percent.

26. *What percentage are black?*

Most of the rest.

27. *What percentage are Oriental?*

Only ten or twelve men.

28. *What other racial groups do you have as customers?*

None I can think of.

Sources of Contacts

The questions in this block are intended to establish the respondent's sources of contacts; they may be phrased:

29. *How many of your tricks were introduced to you by friends?*

30. *Have you ever been a madam?*

31. *Have you worked in a house?*

32. *Have you worked on the street?*

33. *On the street, what percent accept your invitation?*

34. *How often do men who reject your approach cause trouble?*

35. *Have you been a call girl?*

Example of Responses and Coding

Female, age 35

29. *How often do you have tricks that are personal introductions to you by friends?*

Oh, just a few of them.

30. *Have you ever worked as a madam?*

No, but I'm thinking about it.

31. *Have you ever worked in a house?*

Yes, for three years.

32, 35. *Has most of your hustling been done on the street or as a call girl?*

About five years as a call girl and the rest on the street.

33. *When you hustle on the street, what percentage of the time do you get turned down?*

Almost never. You get to know when to make the pitch and when not to, so I'd say very few times.

34. *Has that ever caused any trouble, when you get turned down?*

No, I just keep on walking.

COLUMN III

Petting Techniques—Prostitute Active

This block is concerned with what the prostitute does with her trick. Although the activities are referred to as petting techniques, the behaviors include any sexual stimulation of the partner short of intercourse itself. The fifteen items in the top block of the column all involve the prostitute's behavior toward the partner who is paying for the encounter:

1. Kiss
2. Tongue kiss
3. Body kiss
4. Tongue bath
5. Hand on nipple
6. Mouth on nipple
7. Hand on scrotum
8. Mouth on scrotum
9. Hand on penis
10. Mouth on penis
11. Ejaculate in oral-genital
12. Swallow semen
13. Rimming
14. Flagellation
15. Bondage and discipline

As in the Sex History Inventory itself, the petting technique questions can be asked in checklist fashion, and the interviewer may want to assume that all behaviors are engaged in and ask the questions in a "telling" form. That is:

1. *You kiss the client?*

2. *Is there tongue-kissing?*

3. *You kiss the client's body?*

4. *You give a tongue bath?*

5. *You put your hand on his nipples?*

6. *You put your mouth on his nipples?*

7. *You put your hand on his scrotum?*

8. *You put your mouth on his scrotum?*

9. *You put your hand on his penis?*

10. *You put your mouth on his penis?*

    or

    You put his penis in your mouth?

11. *How often do clients ejaculate in your mouth?*

12. *What percent of the time do you swallow the semen?*

13. *You lick the client's anus (rimming)?*

14. *You whip or flog your customers?*

15. *You bind or tie your customers up and discipline them?*

Petting Techniques—Prostitute Passive

The petting techniques identified in this block are activities that the clients or customers do to the prostitute:

16. Nude body contact
17. Kiss
18. Tongue kiss
19. Hand on nipple/breast
20. Mouth on nipple/breast, orgasm
21. Hand on genitals, orgasm
22. Mouth on genitals, orgasm
23. Rimming
24. Anal intercourse and frequency
25. Flagellation and bondage and discipline
26. Average frequency of orgasm

In addition to identifying what those activities are, the questions also attempt to determine the frequency of orgasm in the prostitute as a result of specific activities performed by the customer. This section provides some interesting insights into the lifestyle of prostitution and its potentially pleasurable benefits.

FIGURE 30-5

		III		
		×		
		×		
		±		
		×—		
		--		
		×		
		×—		
		×		
		✓		
		— if pay		
		✓		
		spt		
		×		
		×		
		× try		
		✓		
		×		
		×		
		✓		
		—, × cli		
		✓ — cli		
		✓ ✓ cli		
		—		
		×		
		×		
		20%		
		✓		
		20%		
		—		
		×		
		×		
		—		
		—		

Examples of Responses and Coding

A. *Female, age 35, prostitute active (see Figure 30-5 for coding of Column III responses)*

1. *Now, with your tricks, is there kissing sometimes?*

   No, I try to avoid kissing if I can.

2. *Is there tongue-kissing?*

   No, I won't allow that.

3. *You kiss their bodies?*

   Yeah, sometimes I do that.

4. *You give a tongue bath?*

   No, I don't like that particularly.

   Have you ever done a tongue bath?

   Oh, once or twice.

5. *You put your hand on their nipples or on their breasts?*

   No, not very often.

6. *Or your mouth on their breasts?*

   No, I don't do that either.

7. *You put your hand on their scrotum?*

   Not if I can avoid it.

8. *Your mouth on their scrotum?*

   No.

9. *You put your hand on their penis?*

   Oh yeah, I try to get it up for them.

10. *And how often do you go down on them?*

    Well, for an extra price I will, but I try to avoid that too.

11. *Do they sometimes ejaculate when you go down on them?*

    Oh yeah.

12. *And do you swallow semen?*

No, I always spit it out.

13. *Do you rim sometimes? Do you put your mouth on their anus?*

No, I avoid that.

15. *Have you ever gotten into S/M—into bondage and discipline?*

Oh, a couple of my weird tricks tried that but I won't have any part of that. It's a bad way to go.

14. *How about whipping them?*

No.

B. *Female, age 35, prostitute passive*

16. *Do you take your clothes off when you have intercourse with a trick?*

Yeah, usually.

17–18. *And you say there isn't any kissing or tongue-kissing if you can avoid it?*

That's right.

19. *How often do the tricks put their hand on your breast?*

Oh, they're always grabbing—so most of them do.

20. *How about their mouth on your breast?*

Yeah, a few of them do that.

Does that ever make you come?

No.

21. *Do they put their hand on your sex organs sometimes?*

Yeah.

And does that ever make you come?

Yeah, a few times it has.

22. *How often do they go down on you?*

More often than you'd think. They do that quite a bit.

And do you ever come off that way?

Oh yeah, that really feels good. I enjoy that.

23. *Do they rim you?*

Oh, once in a while.

24. *And how about anal intercourse?*

No, I absolutely won't permit that.

25-26. *And you said there wasn't any bondage or flagellation. How often do you suppose you come off in the course of a week with a trick?*

Oh, maybe 20 percent of the time.

Positions

The following information is sought in this block:

27. Male above
28. Female above
29. Side
30. Sitting
31. Standing
32. "69"
33. Rear entry

Example of Responses and Coding

Female, age 35

27. *When you have intercourse, is the male usually on top?*

Yeah, most of the time.

28. *And how about you on top?*

Oh, maybe 20 percent of the time.

29. *And on your side?*

Not very often.

30. *When you're sitting?*

No.

31. *Standing?*

No.

32. *How about "69"?*

Yeah, that occurs every once in a while.

33. *How about doing it dog-fashion, from behind?*

I don't really like that so we don't do much of that.

COLUMN IV

Group Sexual Behavior

Group sexual behavior in prostitution can involve two situations: the client may hire two prostitutes at the same time, or the prostitute may have a group party of clients paying for her services. For the purposes of this inventory, both are considered group sex (more than two people).

The questions in this block identify the prostitute's age when group sexual involvement occurred, the frequency with which the activities were experienced, the number of people involved, the activities, the money paid, and the reactions of the prostitute to this behavior:

1. Age of prostitute
2. Frequency
3. Number of people in group and sex
4. Activities
5. Money paid
6. Psychological reactions

The questions asked in sequential order are:

1. *At what age did you begin group sex activities with your clients?*

2. *How frequently have you been involved in group sex activities with clients or with other prostitutes?*

3. *How many people have been in the group?*

4. *What kinds of activities are you involved in during group sex?*

5. *How much money are you paid?*

6. *How do you feel about group sex activities?*

Exhibitionism

Questions on exhibitionism explore the prostitute's experience with exhibitionism—that is, when the prostitute is hired for the specific purpose of putting on a sexual exhibition—as follows:

7. Ages
8. Psychological reaction first time
9. Psychological reaction subsequent times
10. Frequency
11. Money paid: range, average
12. Audience size

Questions are asked in the following ways:

7. *How young were you the first time you worked as an exhibitionist?*

8. *How did you feel the very first time you worked as an exhibitionist?*

9. *How do you feel now about performing in exhibitionistic activities?*

10. *How often have you given exhibitions?*

    What is the total number of exhibitions you have given?

11. *What is the least amount of money you've ever been paid for an exhibition?*

    and

    What is the most you've ever been paid for an exhibition?

    and

    What is your average payment for an exhibition?

12. *How many people are usually in the audience when you give an exhibition?*

Income from Prostitution

Questions about income from prostitution elicit both the average rates of income and the percentages of disbursement for the prostitute as follows:

13. Income range
14. Average money per trick
15. Average money per week
16. Average money per month
17. Average money per year

18. Percent money given to house
19. Percent money given to procurer
20. Police payoffs
21. Frequency of rolling tricks

Questions, asked in sequence, are:

13. *What is the most money you have ever been paid by a trick?*

    and

    What is the least amount of money you have ever been paid by a trick?

14. *How much money do you average per trick?*

15. *How much money do you average per week from prostitution?*

16. *How much money do you average per month?*

17. *How much money do you average per year?*

The interviewer may need to help the respondent in estimating these averages. Getting these averages per week, month and year helps to provide a cross-check, as respondents tend to exaggerate the amount of income a great deal.

Questions 18 through 20 concern payoffs:

18. (If the respondent is a house prostitute.) *What percentage of the payment goes to the house?*

19. (If the respondent is a streetwalker or call girl.) *What percentage of the payment goes to the pimp or agent?*

20. *What percentage of money goes to the police for allowing you to hustle?*

Question 21 is concerned with the prostitute's history of rolling tricks, or robbing the customers. A good cross-reference for this question is the question in the Ages and Relationships block of Column II on how many tricks return two or more times to the same prostitute.

21. *How frequently do you roll your tricks?*

   What's the most you've ever gotten from rolling a trick?

      and

   What's the least amount you've ever gotten from rolling a trick?

Examples of Responses and Coding

A. *Female, age 35, group sex (See Figure 30-6 for coding of Column IV responses)*

   What sort of group sex have you had in your life?

   Well, three or four times, men have wanted me with another girl, and it pays well, so I've done that a few times.

1. *When was the first time that happened?*

   Oh, I was about 19.

2. *And how often have you done that?*

   Uh, oh, maybe a dozen times.

3. *And what was the largest number of people in the group?*

   There's only been three of us. Never had anything larger than that.

4. *What did you do?*

   First the man would ball one of us and then the other, and occasionally he would try to get us together—the other girl and me—and that's happened a few times.

5. *How much do you get paid for this?*

   Oh, well, usually $100 a session.

6. *How do you feel about it?*

   Look, if the money's right, it's all right.

B. *Female, age 35, exhibitionism*

7. *Have you ever given sex shows where you exhibited yourself for an audience?*

   Sure, that has happened.

8. *How did you feel about it the first time?*

   I was embarassed.

9. *After that, how did you feel?*

   I quickly got used to it.

FIGURE 30-6

			IV	
			19	
			12x	
			3 = 2♀	
			c+♀1+	
			100	
			OK	
			19	
			aml	
			OK	
			3-4x	
			100-300	
			4-10	
			$200 - $10	
			$50	
			$750	
			$2000	
			$20,000	
			50%	
			x f ✓ xlike	
			$10 $20	
			— $500	
			X	
			X knw	
			±	
			4x $100 fine	
			5% cond.	
			✓	
			✓ bf	
			X	
			✓ ¼ VD exam	

10. *How often have you been in an exhibition?*

    Three or four times.

11. *How much money have you gotten?*

    One to three hundred dollars.

12. *How large has the audience been?*

    Oh, four to ten men.

C. *Female, age 35, income*

13. *What's the most you've ever gotten for a trick?*

    I'd say $200.

    And what's the least you've ever gotten?

    10.

14. *What do you suppose you average per trick?*

    My regular price is $50.

    And you usually get your regular price?

    Yeah, most of the time.

15. *So, if you earn $50 a trick and you're turning fifteen tricks a week, you're earning about $750 a week.*

    Gee, is it that much? I guess that's right.

16. *Does that mean you earn $3,000 a month?*

    No, it's more like $2,000 a month.

17. *So, perhaps you make $24,000 a year?*

    Well, it's more like $20,000.

18. *When you worked in a house, what percent did the house take?*

    50 percent.

19. *Do you work with a pimp?*

    No, I did for a while, but, boy, they're bad news, so I've given them up.

20. *How much do you have to pay off to the police?*

    Oh, you have to keep the police happy so I'll give them $10 or $20 every so often, whenever they ask for it.

21. *How often do you roll your tricks?*

    I *never* roll a trick.

    Then why do a third of your tricks see you only once?

    Well, once in a while, if he's drunk, I might roll him.

    How much have you gotten by rolling tricks?

    Up to $500.

Social Involvements

The questions in this block reflect a history of difficulties the respondent has had with friends, family, and police as a result of being a prostitute. The questions, asked sequentially are:

22. *What difficulties have you had with friends over your being a prostitute? Have you lost friends because of it?*

23. *What difficulties have you had with relatives, including your parents, over hustling?*

24. *What difficulties have you had with the police?*

25. *Have you ever been arrested? If so, what happened?*

Prophylaxis and Contraception

These questions are concerned with contraception and measures used to control sexually transmitted diseases. The questions asked are:

26. *What percentage of your tricks wear condoms?*

27. *Do you examine the man's penis by pulling back the foreskin and checking for pus?*

28. *Do you wash the man's penis after intercourse?*

29. *Have you ever gotten pregnant with a trick?*

30. *How frequently do you get an exam for sexually transmitted diseases?*

Examples of Responses and Coding

A. *Female, age 35, social involvements*

22. *Have you ever had any trouble with your friends over hustling?*

    No, practically all my friends are in the life.

23. *How about your family?*

They don't know about it. I moved away from home.

24. *What trouble with the police?*

Oh, I've been hassled a few times, particularly when I didn't pay up.

25. *How many times have you been arrested?*

Actually arrested, maybe four times.

And what happened when you got arrested?

I got fined $100 or thirty days in jail, so I paid the $100.

B. *Female, age 35, prophylaxis and contraception*

27. *Do you examine your tricks for VD?*

Yes, if they have a sore on their dick I refuse them. Also if they have a drip after I strip them I refuse or make them use a rubber.

28. *Do you wash the man's penis before or after he has intercourse?*

Yes, before.

26. *What percentage of the men use rubbers?*

Very few of them. Maybe 5 percent.

29. *You ever get pregnant with your tricks?*

No, I never have.

30. *What else do you do to prevent VD?*

I usually douche every day for keeping clean. And I go to the doctor once a month to get checked up.

COLUMN V: SOCIAL-SEXUAL BACKGROUND AND ATTITUDES

The questions in this column identify the prostitute's attitudes about the profession. The questions asked are:

1. *Do you enjoy the variety in terms of partners and methods of having sex that prostitution affords you?*

2. *Have you ever regretted hustling?*

3. *Have you stopped hustling? and, if so, when?*

4. *Are you currently hustling?*

5. *Will you continue to hustle in the future?*

6. *What do you see as the main factor that accounts for your becoming a prostitute?*

7. *What do you see as the reasons for continuing in prostitution?*

The following are commonly cited as important factors in both beginning and continuing prostitution:

   a. Easy money, frequently in abundance
   b. Indolent and relaxed lifestyle
   c. Culture—i.e., "It's a part of the world that I'm in. My friends hustle, and it's a whole way of living."
   d. Sexual variety in partners and techniques
   e. Opportunity to meet different and exciting people

With the exception of money—the major reason cited—these factors are not listed in any order of importance.

8. *What effects will prostitution have on marriage for you?*

9. *If a young person came to you and said that she had just begun hustling and wanted your advice as to whether to continue, what advice would you give?*

Example of Responses and Coding

Female, age 35, social-sexual background (see Figure 30-7 for coding of Column V responses)

17. *What are the reasons for your being in prostitution?*

Well, it's just good money is all.

Outside of money, what other reasons are there for hustling for you?

Oh, I like the variety that you get, you get to see so many different men. And of course the payment I mentioned. It's sort of an exciting lifestyle. You don't know where you're going to end up the next day, and you can be lazy. I can get up late in the mornings. So it's really a pretty good life.

2. *Have you ever regretted it?*

No, I never really have.

3. *Do you think you'll stop?*

Yeah, I want to be a madam, and I think maybe I'll stop hustling on the street before long. I've had about enough of it.

9. *If a young girl had just started hustling, and wanted your advice as to whether she should continue, what would you tell her?*

I'd tell her to get a good training and go ahead.

FIGURE 30-7

				$\mathbb{V}$
				✓
				✗
				✓ soon
				$ + var
				ok if train

Index